# TO HAVE AND TO HOLD
## FUTURE OF A CONTESTED LANDSCAPE

# TO HAVE AND TO HOLD
## FUTURE OF A CONTESTED LANDSCAPE

Edited by Gerrie van Noord

Published by
NVA
Glasgow

and

Luath Press Ltd
Edinburgh

# Contents

# A Realm of Possibilities
## Gerrie van Noord

'The ruin appears to point to a deep and vanished past whose relics merely haunt the present revealing a fading utopian inheritance that barely hangs onto its potential for collective aspiration.'
(Brian Dillon, 'Decline and Fall', *frieze*, issue 130, April 2010)

The first time I visited the former Kilmahew estate together with Angus Farquhar, NVA's creative director, and Rolf Roscher of landscape architects ERZ, who jointly headed the exploration that led to a commission plan for the site, was on a drizzly September day several years ago. It was the landscape, dissected and cut into by two burns, which made an impression first. What struck me throughout our extensive meandering, climbing over and wading through, was that nothing really seemed to be what it had been, in a far and distant past, or even in a more recent one. The entrance to the site was not really an entrance anymore, the paths not really paths, what used to be a garden was a garden no more, a castle no longer a castle, and so on. The sense of having been deserted, left to its own devices, pervaded the entire woodlands, and – inevitably – also the remains of what once was a seminary building.

It was late summer 2010 when the Scottish Government invited public arts organisation NVA to organise a Scottish contribution to the 12th Architecture Biennale in Venice. The impetus for the invitation came from said commission plan for the former Kilmahew estate and remains of the St Peter's Seminary, as presented by NVA earlier in 2010. Located between the villages of Renton and Cardross in West Scotland and completed in 1966 by Gillespie, Kidd & Coia, the seminary building has by some been hailed as a late-modernist masterpiece. Nearly three decades of abandon have, however, reduced it to a ruinous state, and some would like to see the 'carbuncle' demolished sooner rather than later.

The commission plan was the result of several years of intense mapping and exploration of the site and a careful consideration of what its future can hold.

A public realm approach followed a host of failed attempts by planners and developers whose focus was to first and foremost preserve the buildings. The difference of the current plans is that the emphasis is not placed on these buildings, and specifically the seminary, but on the site as a whole and the landscape in which they reside.

Rather than presenting an exhibit in Venice, NVA chose to invite a range of professionals – from landscape architects, geographers, architects and architecture historians, to directors of rural arts organisations, policy makers, arts consultants and writers – to discuss some of the issues that such a site throws up.

A screening of filmmaker Murray Grigor's seminal film *Space and Light*, shot in 1972 when the seminary building was a working space, synchronised with a shot-for-shot recreation of the original in the ruined building, *Space and Light Revisited*, filmed in 2009, formed the backdrop and set the tone for the gathering during a blustery weekend in

November 2010. The context of the Biennale re-connected the discussion about Kilmahew / St Peter's with the radical roots of Ruskin's nineteenth-century conservation theories and the legacies of the likes of Carlo Scarpa's fusion of ancient and modern elements that are evident around Venice. A comparison with one of Scotland's other iconic twentieth-century buildings, the Glasgow School of Art, was made to try and learn from Steven Holl's design for a new school building that will sit directly opposite the iconic original.

The debate in Venice was not an endpoint, but rather the starting point for a deliberately discursive approach, which is intended to open up and expand in and beyond this publication. If anything, it is meant to convey a sense of open-endedness, of potential, and of there not necessarily being a single clear trajectory ahead, but rather a multitude of small, incremental decisions that come together in a continuous, generative sequence.

In our goal-oriented day-to-day realities, it is all too tempting to expect a clear blueprint that covers in

great detail what exactly will be cleared off-site, what will be kept and in what state, and what will be restored and to what level. It is, however, a sense of exploration, a thinking out loud, sometimes by individuals, sometimes by whole groups of people, sometimes coming from one particular field or specialism, sometimes from a combination of fields of expertise and experience, that sits at the core of NVA's approach to Kilmahew / St Peter's.

So, if not a clear trajectory, what does this book contain? For those unfamiliar with the background of the site and its buildings, there is a brief historical overview and a map with a series of location references that engage either with the site's history, or with its landscape features. It also gathers points of view and opinions and notions of best practice, and shifts therein, about preservation and conservation. It does so partly through quotes from the debate as it took place in Venice, but also through a text from John Allan of Avanti Architects, who in 2008 produced the most comprehensive overview to date of the remains of buildings, and

through essays by Gordon Murray and Edward Hollis.

One of the observations made during the conversation in Venice was that if St Peter's had been built in an urban context, it would have vanished because economic arguments would have made it disappear long ago. It is exactly the building's location in a landscape, in the grounds of an estate that has a history of its own, and that harbours remains of a range of other buildings, that has allowed for it to be saved from demolition and for a slow decay to set in over time. And it is exactly the landscape – partly laid out in the nineteenth century, but based on many centuries of previous occupation and use – that offers the potential for new approaches to the site as a whole, and that to a large extent will determine what happens in the future. This potential of the landscape is further elaborated on by Rolf Roscher, and also by Tilman Latz, a German landscape architect whose firm has pioneered new approaches to a range of abandoned locations across Europe and elsewhere. Hayden

Lorimer adds his own interpretation from an entirely different perspective. In a more exploratory manner, artist Emma Cocker has come up with a fictional programme that is actually placed within the Kilmahew estate.

There are of course also thoughts about what can happen in concrete terms. Not least through a summary of the key points derived from NVA's commission plan in the Statement of Intent, but also through the structure of the Venice debate, and responses from those who live nearest, in Renton and Cardross, and from people who grew up close by and for whom the estate and its buildings are not only interwoven with their personal history, but also their personal future.

Alongside all this sit several contributions from authors who have not necessarily visited the woodlands and its buildings on the fringes of Greater Glasgow, but whose writing and research resonates with the vision embedded in the plans. Jane Rendell's text, for instance, highlights that interest

for the issues at stake here is not limited to Scotland, or even the UK, but resonates well beyond.

While many historic landmarks and buildings have been (re)discovered and carefully restored and made accessible to the public all across the UK, and some National Trust managed properties and estates have flourished in recent decades, the fate of many buildings of more recent times, and particularly those built in the second half of the twentieth century, is much less certain. The attention for these buildings, many of which were built in the modernist tradition of form follows function, has noticeably increased in recent years. It is often their almost unavoidable fate – the threat of the demolition hammer after years of use with only basic maintenance and care (or sometimes pure lack thereof) – and their common perception as trouble spots that has sparked renewed interest in what they are and what they stand for.

The thought-provoking Venice exhibit entitled *Cronocaos* by Rem Koolhaas and his OMA / AMO

office drew attention to a general failing to deal with the architectural legacy of the second half of the twentieth century on a global scale. Preceding rafts of images (which included St Peter's) and other references to a wide range of (late) modernist buildings, the presentation was framed by the following statement:

'At its moment of surreptitious apotheosis, preservation does not quite know what to do with its empire. As the scale and importance of preservation escalates each year, the absence of a theory and a lack of interest invested in this seemingly remote domain becomes dangerous. The current moment has almost no idea of how to negotiate the coexistence of radical change and radical stasis going into the future.'

Where are we now with Kilmahew / St Peter's? An offer to buy from NVA to the Archdiocese of Glasgow – the current owners of the site – has been accepted. The organisation has given itself two years to raise the funds and come up with a feasible plan to save the buildings and to start to transform the wider setting. A core aim is to establish a nationally placed research, learning and cultural programme using the site as subject. Of course, they won't do that on their own: many stakeholders and parties are already actively involved in discussions and explorations. There is a lot of 'collective aspiration' that has the potential to maybe even invert the bankruptcy of the utopian ideology that has given rise to so much material in the first place. What is certain is that a whole realm of possibilities is only just beginning to open up.

# The History of Kilmahew / St Peter's

## Early History

The name 'Kilmahew' is derived from the chapel of St Mahew (or Mochta), shown on early maps on a piece of land called the 'Kirkton of Kilmahew', located close to the Clyde estuary. The chapel is said to have existed since earliest Christian times, with 'Kil' referring to its Celtic origins.

The first documented reference to a Napier owning the land (and being in Scotland) is in two charters issued by Malcolm, Earl of Lennox, who lived at the end of the thirteenth century. The reference is to John Napier, who was granted 'all that quarter of lands called Kylmethew lying between Muydugwen and Archerreran' in one of the charters. The full extent of the grounds cannot be determined exactly, but a 'quarter-land' is likely to have equalled 26 Scots acres (32.5 Imperial acres or 13.26 hectares). One of John's descendants, William Napier, added more land to the estate, which included the chapel, in the fourteenth century. By the mid-fifteenth century it must have been in ruins because there are records that it was rebuilt in 1467 by the then Laird of Kilmahew, Duncan Napier.

Some modern-day accounts suggest that the tower house, or keep, known as 'Kilmahew Castle', was built in the fifteenth century, while some say the fifteenth and seventeenth centuries. An Archaeological Assessment concluded that the first development phase probably dates from the sixteenth century, with subsequent major work taking place in the mid to late eighteenth century and late eighteenth, early nineteenth centuries.*

## Eighteenth and Nineteenth Centuries

George Maxwell Napier inherited Kilmahew in 1694 and it is his name that is associated with the decline of the Napiers of Kilmahew. He was unusually extravagant and as a result started to sell off land to settle his debts as early as 1705, and again in 1721 and 1735. Local myth has it that his favourite horse is buried near a waterfall in the glen of Kilmahew.

The Roy's Map, which dates back to the 1750s, clearly shows the location of the two burns that cross the site – the Kilmahew Burn and the Wallaceton Burn – as they join before flowing South to the Clyde estuary. The same map shows a

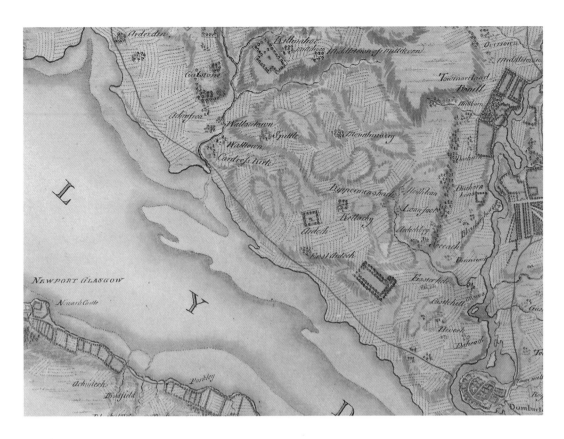

rectilinear 'emparked' area, enclosed by park paling, to the North of the 'triangle' created by their union. A house or 'castle' occupies a central position within the enclosure, surrounded by formal landscape. North of the paling lies an informal settlement called 'Milldovan'. In later maps this house is referred to as the 'Triangle of Milndovan'.

When George Napier died in 1744, all of his children had predeceased him, so what he hadn't squandered yet passed, after some contestation, to Jean Smith (Napier), a distant relative via the line of John Maxwell (George's second brother). Two generations later, the eighteenth Laird of Kilmahew, William Napier, an American citizen, decided to make up and sell the titles to what little remained of the estate in 1820.

Mr Sharp (married to William Napier's sister) bought the estate, and promptly sold it to his brother Alexander Sharp. Arthur Jones, author of Cardross: The Village in Days Gone By (1985), records that Alexander Sharp had the 'castle' altered to make it habitable. However, the Archaeological Assessment

suggests that the last major work to Kilmahew Castle probably took place earlier than this. Although all of Sharp's children are recorded as born here, the family's principal residence was elsewhere.

In 1848 James Burns acquired Bloomhill, which lies due South of Kilmahew. Over the next decade or so, Burns gradually bought up what is believed to be the original estate of Kilmahew in no less than eight portions. Burns had made his money in steam navigation, and, in conjunction with his brother George, was one of the founders of the Cunard shipping line.

Between 1865 and 1868 Burns' son, John William Burns, commissioned the architect John Burnet to design and build a new mansion house at Kilmahew. It was thought to be a fine example of the Scots Baronial merged with the Jacobean type. The house was surrounded by a broad terrace and formal garden, sited in a sheltered situation to the East of Kilmahew burn. Built from greenish-grey stone, hewn from a local quarry, its peaked gables and lofty turrets, with panoramic views from the upper

storeys, could be seen from the Clyde rising above the wooded glens.

After his father's death, John Burns began an extensive scheme of improvements, including road building, fencing and draining. He also continued to add land to the estate, including that around the old chapel. Boundaries were removed and the surrounding farmland was planted as parkland. There were two lodges, West Lodge and South Lodge, a stable complex with coach house, and a large kitchen garden with glasshouses, bothies, etc. The main approach was via a new drive from the West over a new stone Gothic bridge. The South approach drive crossed a double stone bridge spanning the two burns. An intricate network of paths, including at least eleven footbridges, enabled the visitor to explore the two glens.

Features included a new artificial lake, curling pond and, of course, the ruins of Kilmahew Castle or Keep, by this time serving as an architectural curiosity or folly that must have held huge attraction to the Victorians. The glen was left in its natural state, its

banks embellished with ornamental trees and shrubs that accentuated its picturesque qualities, some of which were said to have been collected by Burns thanks to his Cunard connections. In places, the existing wooded areas were expanded to screen new developments such as the lake and stables so that from most open areas everything appeared swathed in woodland. The family opened the grounds regularly to visitors and the gardens were much admired. John Fleming was gardener throughout much of the Victorian period, while David Morris was the gardener from the end of the nineteenth century onwards.

## Twentieth Century

In 1900 John William Burns' son inherited the estate, but eight years later he leased it to Claud Allan, and in 1919 the estate was advertised for sale. At this time it amounted to 1,552 acres, which was to be sold in lots and included the old castle or keep, the mansion house and grounds, Asker Farm with Asker Hill rough pasture and plantation, Kilmahew Farm, Kilmahew Cottages, Low Milndovan Farm,

Auchenfroe House and grounds with about an acre of woodland and a cottage, and Bloomhill House and grounds. After having leased it for over a decade, it was Allan who bought the estate.

It was probably also Allan who continued modernisation, including a sewage plant, stables, a gasometer that replaced the coach house, and a new, more direct road linking the stables to the house. Views were opened up East of the house, while the woodland was extended eastwards, to screen new tennis courts. The gardens continued to be well maintained and appreciated. At this time, the head gardener was Frank G. Dunbar, relatively well known for his contributions to *The Gardeners' Chronicle*. An account of a visit to the gardens from 1938 describes them in some detail, noting that 'An interesting feature of the garden is that the natural effect has been closely adhered to, even to the extent of planting, for the most part, only shrubs and trees as are in true keeping with the whole conception.'

World War II inflicted considerable damage to the entire site, after which the Archdiocese of Glasgow acquired the estate in 1948. The church's St Peter's College came from the neighbouring property of Darleith, and, having settled down there, looked around for means of expansion and for increasing student accommodation. The house at Darleith was given over to the students of philosophy and Kilmahew was reserved for the theological students. But the compact, vertical plan of Kilmahew House was not so easily adapted to the requirements of college life.

In 1953, the Archdiocese approached Gillespie, Kidd & Coia, with whom they already had a professional relationship, to consider an extension to Kilmahew. The diocese required accommodation for 115 students, classrooms, a library, a dining area, a chapel, a convent block and a swimming pool. The swimming pool was later deleted from the brief, and the accommodation reduced to 100 trainee priests. The diocese introduced Father David McRoberts, who had developed a scheme to extend the existing house, to Coia. McRoberts' proposal included a new sisters' wing to the North, a library and dining room to the North-West and a student block to the South-West. This scheme was eventually shelved due to other financial commitments of the diocese.

When the diocese came to review the scheme again, Gillespie, Kidd & Coia had evolved and Isi Metzstein and Andy MacMillan had joined the practice. In 1959 a completely new design was accepted and developed in 'close and exclusive collaboration with the Archbishop – not with anyone else, just the Archbishop himself'. The proposals were further developed, with certain changes made, and construction was planned to commence in 1961 and to be completed in the spring of 1963.

After significant delay, due to weather and poor ground conditions that required redesign and additional work, the students and staff finally took possession of the new college on 1 October 1966. The last internal finishing works were completed in 1968.

The college was only occupied for fourteen years, as the diocese took the decision to close St Peter's Seminary in 1979 and it finally closed in 1980. The reasons attributed to the closure of the seminary were changes to the curriculum as a result of the Second Vatican Council, decreasing numbers of ordination, financial difficulties of the Church, as well as the perceived defects of the building.

In 1983 the Church decided to use the buildings as a drug rehabilitation and detoxification centre, which was organised by the Church social services department and run for five years. The centre was then closed in 1987, due to ongoing problems with the deterioration of the building's fabric. The diocese submitted several applications for demolition, all of which were refused. Since then a series of planning and listed building applications have been submitted and refused.

Despite attempts to secure the buildings effectively, extensive vandalism and theft occurred over time. Having suffered two fires had left Kilmahew House in a dangerous condition and it was subsequently demolished in 1995. In 1993 the Secretary of State listed the Coia Buildings as of special architectural importance, Category 'A'.

This in an abridged version of the site history derived from the 2008 Avanti report 'St Peter's Seminary, Cardross'. For the full version, as well as a detailed chronology with regards to the actual building of the seminary, please see http://www.historic-scotland.gov.uk/index/news/indepth/stpeters/stpeters-avantireport.htm

The site history appears in section 12, as part of the appendices, on pp. 263-70. A detailed chronology can be found on pp. 282-91.

*The Archaeological Assessment is part of the Avanti report, and can be found on pages 271-81 (section 12).

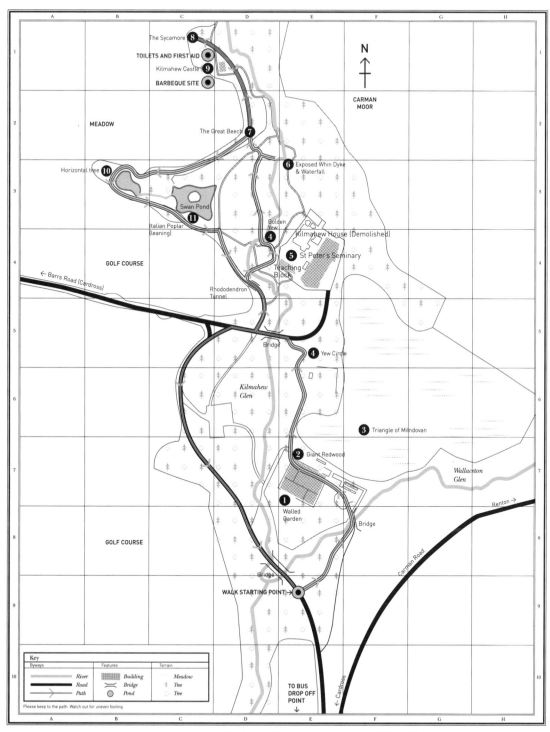

The Sycamore ⑧
**TOILETS AND FIRST AID** ⦿
Kilmahew Castle ⑨
**BARBEQUE SITE** ⦿

N ↑

CARMAN MOOR

MEADOW

The Great Beech ⑦

Exposed Whin Dyke ⑥
& Waterfall

Horizontal tree ⑩

Swan Pond

Italian Poplar
(leaning)              ⑪

Golden
Yew

Kilmahew House (Demolished)
④
St Peter's Seminary
⑤
Teaching
Block

Rhododendron
Tunnel

← Barrs Road (Cardross)

GOLF COURSE

Bridge

Yew Circle ④

*Kilmahew
Glen*

Triangle of Milndovan ③

Giant Redwood ②

① 

Walled
Garden

*Wallaceton
Glen*

Renton →

Carman Road

Bridge

GOLF COURSE

Bridge

**WALK STARTING POINT** →⦿

← Cardross

**Key**

| Byways | | Features | | Terrain | |
|---|---|---|---|---|---|
| | *River* | ▨ | *Building* | | *Meadow* |
| | *Road* | ✕ | *Bridge* | | *Tree* |
| | *Path* | ◯ | *Pond* | | *Tree* |

Please keep to the path. Watch out for uneven footing

TO BUS
DROP OFF
POINT
↓

Exploring Kilmahew walk, October 2010, with temporary signage and bridge

# ❶ Walled Gardens

The walled gardens were formerly the kitchen gardens for Kilmahew House. They were inaugurated in 1866, having been set out by John Fleming, a renowned gardener of the time, who had previously worked at Cliveden House, in Berkshire, along the Thames. He used the glasshouse, built by Glasgow company Simpson & Farmer, as a research base and went on to write *A Treatise on the Vine, Pine-apple, Peach, Plum and Nectarine &C*, which was published in 1872. David Morris took over as estate gardener in the late nineteenth century, introducing a number of exotic tree species from around the world, particularly from Japan. Mr Dunbar, who succeeded him, was famous for his sweet pea growing. During their first hundred years the grounds were often opened up to visitors.

# ❷ Giant Redwood

All the trees noted on the map have been chosen as 'signature' trees, because of either their age or size, and some have been listed officially at www.ancient-tree-hunt.org.uk as veteran trees. The giant sequoia (redwood) was first brought into cultivation in 1853 by Scotsman John D. Matthew, who collected a small quantity of seeds from the Calaveras Grove in California. Commercial distribution soon followed across Europe. The Californian grove, set in the middle altitudes of the Sierra Nevada, became a state park in 1931 and was one of America's first tourist attractions.

# ❸ Triangle of Milndovan

Milndovan is the medieval name for the triangulated area of meadow and farmland that lies between the two burns, Kilmahew Burn and Wallaceton Burn, and is the likely location of an ancient manorial house (long-since destroyed) seen on early maps of the area. There is speculation that this may have been the home of Robert the Bruce in his later years.

# ❹ Yew Circle and Golden Yew

A large number of yew trees, both planted and self-seeded, are thriving throughout the woodlands. The yew is one of Britain's native species and has been considered sacred since pre-Christian times. It has qualities of longevity and regeneration (drooping branches of old yew trees can root and form new trunks where they touch the ground), and thus it came to symbolise death and resurrection. Yew trees have historically been used to make bows because of their wood's strength and flexibility.

# ❺ St Peter's Seminary

The Archdiocese of Glasgow acquired the estate in 1948 and Kilmahew House was subsequently brought into use for theological students. The architects Gillespie, Kidd & Coia were approached in 1953 to consider an extension to Kilmahew House. This evolved into the radical modernist design by Andy MacMillan and Isi Metzstein for a new set of buildings wrapped around the existing house. Construction started in 1961 and the seminary opened in 1966. The new building was dominated by a stepped, four-storey block of individual bedrooms, creating a dramatic frame for the floating interior spaces of the sanctuary chapel and refectory. The scheme owed its form to the desire to preserve the existing Victorian house with least disturbance and also to the aspiration of giving expression to the unity of the student-priests' lives by integrating all the main spaces into one impressive composition. At right angles to the main building is the teaching block, which incorporated four lecture rooms, a large library and recreation spaces. With its dramatic cantilever reaching West to the main gorge, the building is remarkable for both the boldness of its execution and the austerity of its exposed concrete elements. While giving the appearance of a radical imposition in a romantic setting, it was designed as a practical solution showing sensitivity to the line of the main terraced retaining wall of Kilmahew House, which was destroyed by fire in the early 1990s.

## ❻ Exposed Whin Dyke and Waterfall

The red sandstone, which is revealed in the beds of the burns, was quarried from higher up on Carman Moor and used to build the bridges and infrastructure of the original estate. The Gartness Fault, which runs across the region towards Loch Lomond, reveals itself as bands of igneous and metamorphic rock. The presence of this harder rock gives rise to dramatic waterfalls, which contrast with the more steeply incised character of the gorge that appears downstream.

## ❼ Great Beech

In the mid nineteenth century it was fashionable to plant beech saplings in bundles, so that a number of trunks would rise up and intertwine over time. Kilmahew's largest beech tree is a good example of this tradition.

## ❽ Sycamore

One of the oldest trees on the site, this specimen has a circumference of over four metres. The wonderful spread of upper branches has been achieved through careful 'pollarding' over a century ago. This technique, in which the upper branches of a tree are removed to promote a dense head of foliage and branches, creates a perfectly rounded form.

## ❾ Kilmahew Castle

The fifteenth- / sixteenth-century semi-ruinous castle presents a solid square appearance, with its approximately 100 feet high walls. It was for long periods owned by the Napier family. The structure was styled as a traditional Scottish keep, until the notable intervention of Mr Sharp, owner of the estate in the early nineteenth century, who decided to make the old castle habitable. In further acts of 'follification', he knocked out several windows in the ancient walls, replacing them in the French gothic style. A new entrance was also introduced, flanked with niches for columns on the South-West angle of the wall. The broad lintel over the door at the North-West angle bore the motto 'The Peace of God Be Herein'. It is presumed that he either ran out of money or embraced the fashion for faked ruins prevalent at the time. Towards the end of the Victorian era the castle suffered from a fire and the upper part of the battlements was mostly destroyed.

## ❿ Horizontal Tree

This tree was blown down during the Great Storm of January 1968 and now lies across the Swan Pond. The storm was central Scotland's worst natural disaster since records began, with winds of over 100mph accompanied by tornadoes, damaging 250,000 houses and leaving 20 dead and more than 2,000 people homeless.

## ⓫ Swan Pond

The Swan Pond was constructed for the inhabitants of Kilmahew House in the 1860s. Today wildlife, including newts, toads, frogs, herons and moorhens, is thriving in and around the pond. Pipistrelle bats have been spotted here and in Kilmahew Castle.

# Statement of Intent

'Brutalism with its rough-hewn rawness always was a picture of future ruins. But in fact it is not so much ruined as dormant, derelict – still functioning even in a drastically badly treated fashion and as such ready to be recharged and reactivated.'
Owen Hatherley

## Site as subject

The opportunity to purchase Kilmahew / St Peter's concludes a number of years of speculation about the future of the seminary buildings and marks the beginning of a new vision for the site and the people for whom it has significance.

The Commission Plan produced by NVA in 2010 sets out a variety of options for the transformation of the buildings and 140 acres of semi-ancient woodlands. By working closely with the history and evolution of the site, the work will embrace an incremental process of change that accepts the state of each stage of its resuscitation as complete in itself. This supports the principle of an *unfinished* work and accepts a level of entropy. It critiques any approach to impose a permanent 'solution' to the conflicted history of the twentieth-century buildings and traces of earlier structures within the wider landscape.

The layering of remnants from self-seeded woodland, to medieval castle, to designed landscape, to religious institution, to abandoned realm, to a contemporary modified landscape, reveals ideologies and approaches to design and implementation that are seemingly at odds with each other. The need or desire for privacy versus public accessibility has shifted throughout time. The archaeology of ideas, which have developed over the last two and a half years through investigation, consultation, discussion and imaginative thinking, sets out a vision for a distinctive creative and productive landscape.

## A Sense of Otherness

Kilmahew / St Peter's is primarily to be accessed on foot. Part of the special atmosphere of the woodlands and double gorge setting comes out of the lack of visual and environmental intrusion by cars. A daily routine envisages opening up the three to four kilometres of paths to free access and encourages movement through the buildings that are part of the former seminary.

## Peripatetic Learning

While the original programme for the seminary was very specific in its links between form and function (a centre of religious learning focused around the delivery of the Roman Catholic Mass), it still offers a dramatic set of spaces that offer unusual ways of framing human activity. Aspects of the social spirit and ambition with which the original commission was undertaken still have clear relevance to a practice-led teaching programme and stand in stark contrast to the pessimism that characterises current times.

## A Sense of Uncertainty

The buildings are seen as an integrated 'artwork' to be experienced as part of a journey between external and internal spaces with minimal intrusion of signage. The emphasis is on maintaining a sense of 'the unknown' and allowing the interaction of features and their interpretation to remain complex, inviting the visitor as an active *protagonist* to return a number of times to 'read' the site as a non-sequential or disrupted narrative. Using techniques of partial disorientation stands in contrast to the presentation of many heritage landscapes and buildings; rather than knowing exactly what you are going to get and rarely having your expectations challenged, here your experience shifts from year to year.

## A Beating Heart

The chapel and sanctuary are made wind- and watertight with the refectory left open to the elements from the side and North elevations. Re-roofing and temporary window protection on the upper floors still allow natural light to penetrate the interior. The radical mixture of consolidated and partially restored forms within the mega-structure promotes a practical rather than purely aesthetic function for the new scheme.

## A Living Heritage

Movement should feel as unrestricted as possible with simple and clean solutions blocking routes to upper floors. A light touch picks up on detailing or materials used in the original design, or finds appropriate contemporary interventions.

An overall masterplan sets out to rescue layers of meaning within the wider landscape through the provision of growing spaces and accommodation alongside a process of path restoration, new build, adaption of older structures, landscape modification and bold intervention to change the hierarchy of routes and hidden qualities that typify the current abandoned woodlands and buildings.

As an Invisible College, Kilmahew / St Peter's seeks to establish a platform for knowledge transfer and experiential teaching in a productive landscape. It will bring together dynamic new thinking and the interchange of ideas outside the limitations of professional and academic 'silos'. The site offers a rich and complex history that provides the source material for a growing body of research, live experimentation and interaction.

Kilmahew / St Peter's will involve key academic and local partners directly in an annual research programme that forms the source material for a series of summer-based public art commissions, provocations and presentations.

## A Radical Rural Arts Practice

Avoiding the potential for institutional inertia means accepting that intellectual currents and perceptions shift over time. The programme will require continual questioning and re-examination of accepted positions and given values. Academics,

landscape architects, activists, artists, architects and farmers, among others, both local and visiting, will contribute to the development of knowledge relevant to generating changing readings of Kilmahew / St Peter's.

On a daily basis the points of engagement and demarcation may be relatively sparse, with the site laid out as a puzzle to be figured out over time. This leaves space for personal responses to natural and introduced phenomena and allows people to make their own set of decisions as they move across the terrain.

Temporary interventions can highlight particular features or routes, with the potential to employ thematic approaches to commissioning that change seasonally or annually. Each influences a different way of seeing or understanding that contrasts with any single-issue reading of landscape.

The principles of the Invisible College accrue around the ideal of affordable and innovative learning for all. The importance of releasing the brilliance of chosen academic partners from university and college settings to share new thinking with a wider public

can become an alternative to traditional tertiary education, which for many will become inaccessible because of cost.

For current arts and humanities research programmes there is a strong desire to reach outside a hermetic reciprocal relationship towards a participating network and to work with new alignments of external partnerships.

By using a model that is *generative* rather than *provision*-based, people of all backgrounds and interests are encouraged to contribute creatively to ideas for development, debate key issues and build involvement in the progress of the creative programme.

Extending the notion of place making through an understanding that the site inspires polarised opinion rather than a homogeneous response, Kilmahew / St Peter's seeks to exploit its contested nature as a key to its future reputation and prominence.

This text is derived from the 2010 Commission Plan and several texts written subsequently.

# Poetry and Pragmatism
## Restoring St Peter's Seminary
### John Allan

Much of the discourse on St Peter's that has accumulated over the years has tended to focus on the elegiac, numinous aspects of this extraordinary site and its 'surviving' buildings and, in the latter case, on the unfamiliar philosophical and cultural challenges of coming to terms with perhaps the first truly authentic modern ruin. At one extreme the case has been argued for extending the process of permissive decay to the point of total atrophy – the ultimate 'do nothing option'. Other, more idealistic or defiant, voices have promoted the cause of recovery, even complete restitution of the original buildings and their setting. There is a poetic dimension to both such propositions, a romantic reflex perhaps induced by the very extremity of dereliction itself. These debates have greatly illuminated modernism's self-interrogation, the process of confronting a present that is now past, 'the future that was', and merge into a larger ongoing project of cultural reconciliation that may ultimately transcend specific reference to the buildings themselves.

Other contributors to this collection of essays will doubtless pursue some of these wider historical and philosophical questions posed by the 'St Peter's phenomenon' – what might be rather loosely termed its poetic dimension – and such deliberations will surely continue to enrich our understanding of the underlying issues. However, as a practising architect leading the professional team committed to undertaking the actual re-building project now being contemplated I intend to focus here rather on the ample pragmatic and practical issues that it presents. My starting point must be the research assignment initiated in 2007 when Avanti Architects and a team of consultants were commissioned jointly by the Archdiocese of Glasgow and Historic Scotland to produce a Conservation Assessment of St Peter's. Completed in 2008, this is the most recent and comprehensive study of the buildings and their site.*

The investigation included an historical account of the seminary and the surrounding estate, a systematic assessment of its heritage significance, a detailed survey of its current condition and necessary remedial works, identification of existing hazards and security issues, and a description

(and costings) of a range of generic options for rehabilitating the buildings and the site that were also compatible with the statement of significance. The range of consultant disciplines in the team enabled the full range of architectural, structural, environmental, archaeological, landscape and financial issues to be addressed. The study also set out a syllabus of actions and management procedures to enable a recovery project to be progressed.

Over the years there has been a trail of unsuccessful proposals for St Peter's, which has only added to its legendary reputation as an elegiac ruin. A key tenet of our study, which was the subject of wide consultation and will now serve as a document of reference, was that it should not easily be invalidated by relying on an unduly ambitious or prescriptive scheme that could quickly be proven unfeasible. Instead it sought for a series of practical strategies whereby modest but worthwhile improvements could be achieved initially, which would not preclude, but rather might stimulate, more ambitious developments later.

This layered approach, with its implied dynamic of 'becoming', remains pivotal to the present context, in which it is clear that any rescue project must not only recognise the many realities and narratives through which St Peter's is apprehended by its diverse audiences, but will also necessarily reflect the technical and financial exigencies of incremental recovery, whereby early stages will inform later ones, the ideal will be tempered by the feasible, and differing contributions (including multiple funding streams) must be assimilated from a range of participants.

Recognition of this unfolding developmental dimension should not be equated with opportunism or uncertainty of motivation. On the contrary, inclusiveness of process can only usefully progress through clarity of the underlying aim. The essential purpose of revitalising St Peter's Seminary, and Kilmahew as a whole, is to return it to beneficial use – both literally in the inhabitation and cultivation of its lands for productive yield, and instrumentally in enabling the buildings and gardens to sustain a wide range of social programmes, whether educational, recreational or cultural – in short to reconstitute the secular import of its original function – that of a college – in its widest possible connotation. To this end the buildings and site will provide a platform – be this constructive in serving various definable operational activities, or inductive by retaining that numinous essence for participants to adumbrate for themselves.

In preparing our response to this new initiative we are acutely aware of the instructive and ethical dimension of the project and the need not only to accomplish an effective rescue of the buildings under consideration, but also to provide an accessible evidence trail of the conservation philosophy and technical toolbox employed in doing so. There is of course no shortage of charters and guidance in such matters, and our work will proceed in full cognisance of these resources. A consistent tenet of such documents is that the criteria adopted in formulating conservation and repair measures are explicitly articulated for the project record, which in itself should be exploited as an extended educational benefit of the enterprise. The 2008 Assessment was itself substantially referenced in this respect.

Here only a generic outline of such a methodology can be indicated, but it should be appreciated that the process of formulating an appropriate response must entail the systematic interrogation of every single element of the complex. The Seminary, the Teaching Block, the Convent, the Kitchen Block, the original Kilmahew House (or rather its remaining outline) constitute a diverse company of architectural personalities that cannot necessarily be addressed in a singular conservation reflex. They will each call for bespoke, differentiated responses. Yet these must equally cohere in the compositional unity that they create as a group that still documents the daily regime of its erstwhile community.

The inquisition requires answers to the recurring questions – Is this element significant? In what does this significance reside? How may its inherent heritage value be best secured? Would restoration measures in a particular instance be evidence-based

or conjectural? If the element in question is not deemed significant, what degree of alteration or intervention is legitimate? When do the demands of new use justify relinquishing a previous one? and so on – in exhaustive individual detail. The causality in reaching an outcome is one of the fascinations of such work, but, however conscientiously undertaken, it is unlikely to be entirely free of controversy – for the unavoidable reason that working with historic buildings and places, like any other branch of architecture or design, inevitably calls for judgement, for deciding priorities. One need only consider the issue of the graffiti, which in the case of St Peter's constitutes such a conspicuous part of its historical patina. To ask simply whether it should be retained or be removed would be to pose the wrong question. Some areas are of certain significance and form a compelling aspect of the buildings' aura. Others are worthless, gratuitous or merely unsightly. It all has to be argued out.

That said, the scope of work may be expected to comprise at least three essential types of activity – repair, upgrade and intervention. Repair constitutes the recovery and making good of original damaged fabric. The intention here is to retrieve and restore any significant original fabric capable of rehabilitation for viable future service. An internal example would be the retention and remediation of selected vaulted ceilings of the trainee priests' cells in cases where it is found possible to work with and consolidate the remaining fabric. An exterior example would be the refurbishment of the highly characteristic pre-cast pebble-faced concrete panels, which form the principal cladding to the seminary and convent block. Even here, however, a distinction must be made between the panels themselves and the means by which they are fixed, a combination of overly slender pre-cast posts and mild steel bolts and cleats, which in most cases is now inadequate, indeed hazardous, and in need of complete re-engineering, using galvanised or stainless steel materials to ensure long-term security and safety of the units.

Upgrade entails the improvement or replacement of fabric or services where the original is no longer

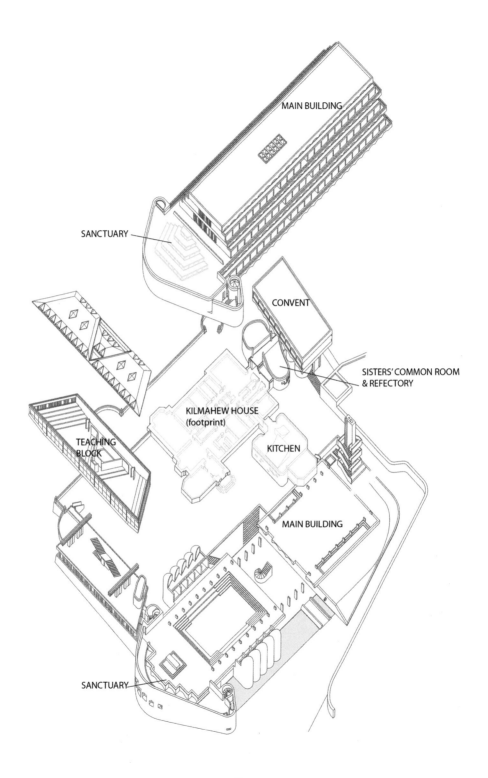

MAIN BUILDING

SANCTUARY

CONVENT

SISTERS' COMMON ROOM
& REFECTORY

KILMAHEW HOUSE
(footprint)

KITCHEN

TEACHING
BLOCK

MAIN BUILDING

SANCTUARY

compliant or fit for purpose. The prime example will be the renewal of service installations where the original systems are deficient, lost or beyond repair – e.g. drainage, electrics, water – or, in the case of the vaulted ceilings noted above, the replacement of a ceiling and its supporting arched metal framework where the original has either collapsed or is irretrievably damaged. Of critical importance in relation to the renewal of services infrastructure will be the exploitation of opportunities offered by the site itself for harnessing green energy and sustainable natural resources.

Intervention will occur where a new use demands an adaptation of the original building arrangement, and, for example, would apply to a proposal to convert the convent block to office use, or if the teaching block were considered for serving a residential function. Most critical perhaps will be the challenge of adapting the chapel and sanctuary, the focus of the former seminary's devotional rituals, to use as an events space capable of accommodating a wide range of secular activities. In such circumstances the key consideration will be to identify the nature and significance of the spaces and structure and assess whether the intervention being contemplated would contradict or be detrimental to that significance.

Alongside these generic considerations, it should be noted that, as the current project scope is unlikely – indeed does not aim – to achieve the complete restitution of the entire seminary complex in a single phase or even at all, certain elements may need to be consolidated in a 'holding operation' until such

time as resources permit further recovery. While the received wisdom of John Ruskin suggests we must not be offended if such 'aids' are 'unsightly', we should also observe the best practice protocol that design of temporary measures should always take due account of the eventual permanent ones. After all, 'temporariness' is itself a relative consideration and entails a careful financial calculus as to the value of investment appropriate for work that by definition should later be revisited – but through change of circumstance may not be after all. Postponement of rebuilding the elaborate (and expensive) pyramidal rooflight over the sanctuary would surely not justify installing an 'unsightly' covering that prevented the introduction of any natural light. It is the admission of light that has priority before the specific means by which it is achieved and even a temporary solution should recognise this.

Our approach to these demands will thus be to tailor each response to reflect the sensitivity of the element concerned. Elements of high sensitivity will require full regard to be paid to the original design, using so far as possible the authentic materials and details on a like-for-like basis. Where repairs are to be carried out locally within a larger surviving field of original fabric, the work would be as closely matched as possible to the original, but still capable of discreet differentiation. In some cases key fragments of original fabric survive to provide templates for replacement – for example the fourteen 'leaf-spring' roof beams over the sanctuary (now all but lost) or the cradle shell eaves headers (fragments of which survive) that ran the length of

the main building ground floor. These will be crucial to achieving authentic reconstruction.

Where the original detail or materials contributed to early failure, or where the type or location of the work is not 'heritage sensitive', the intention is to undertake necessary replacement work with discretion while also ensuring that, wherever possible, critical details are re-formulated in such a way as to provide a more viable outcome. Examples would include the roofs of the main building and convent block, which are not generally visible and which therefore may be discreetly upgraded for better thermal and drainage performance. In such cases a balance must be struck between authentic conservation and constructional prudence. Little purpose is served by faithful replication of a flawed detail if the result will entail further commitment of precious funds for avoidable maintenance in future. Neither for that matter can current standards of compliance, whether this relates to inclusive access, energy efficiency or health and safety, be assumed to be always capable of being side-stepped through special heritage claims or formal derogation. These too must be conscientiously evaluated and a responsible balance struck as and where appropriate.

In addition to field survey of the buildings in their current condition, the repair and restoration proposals will be closely informed by reference to the extensive archive of original drawings in the Gillespie, Kidd & Coia Archive held at the Glasgow School of Art. This considerable cache of material provides an almost comprehensive record of the designers' original intentions, though it should be noted that the drawings as preserved do not always correspond with the building as built. The collection, none the less, offers an extraordinary resource, both for the recovery project and its ensuing use, to enhance the understanding of this unique episode in modern Scottish architecture.

However, the rescue of St Peter's Seminary should reach beyond local or even national boundaries. It promises to be a Modern Movement rescue project of international significance and will take place at a time when the revaluation of modern heritage is at a critical stage. Moreover, the parallel regeneration of its landscape setting will place the recovery of the buildings in a still longer and richer historical perspective.

As Nick Carraway memorably cautioned the Great Gatsby in Scott Fitzgerald's tragic tale, 'you can't repeat the past!' So likewise any progressive conservation project to be sustainable must ultimately entail a transformation. St Peter's promises to do so more than most, not only honouring the poetry of its extraordinary past, but also practically enabling future generations to create new narratives of their own.

* The entire 2008 Avanti report can be downloaded from: http://www.historic-scotland.gov.uk/index/news/indepth/stpeters/stpeters-avantireport.htm

# Beyond Venice
## Gordon Murray

Canaletto and Bellini have documented pictographic representations of Venice. On the other hand, Turner and Whistler captured something more – the light, the dampness, a limpidity – something of Visconti in *Death in Venice*. The city's essence. The theme of the Sejima Biennale in Venice in autumn 2010 was 'People Meet in Architecture'.* A subtext of this might be 'public space as contested space', or, in turn, how do we conserve and safeguard public space in the twenty-first century?

It is appropriate that our discussion was held in Venice, for several reasons. Firstly the Biennale, long the location for serious cultural polemic, originating in the carabinieri marching across St Mark's Square in the late 1970s to quell the protests on the work of Joseph Beuys, as recognised by Aldo Rossi and Paolo Portoghesi when they set up the original. It is also the home of Carlo Scarpa, another polemicist in the lineage of Ruskin who provides useful three-dimensional, critical commentary on the lack of any theoretical approach to conservation. Finally because Venice is the lexicon: it cannot of itself

offer solutions but is a concise version of any basic dictionary of desirable form and space. We made a few friends there too and to have our debate sit alongside OMA and Rem Koolhaas' contribution to the Biennale was both timely and resonant. We are at a crossroads here. I hope this is the start of many similar debates.

John Ruskin argued:
> 'Great nations write their autobiographies in three manuscripts. The book of their deeds, the book of their words, and the book of their arts. Not one of those books can be understood unless we read the others, but of the three, the only quite trustworthy one is the last.'

If 'conservation' as a concept could be said to have started with the radical actions of Ruskin and Count Alvise Zorzi in 1887 at St Mark's Basilica in Venice, then it is timely that we look for new paradigms, new methods and approaches. The conversation in Venice sought to navigate a path towards a new radical view in the manner of Ruskin. This can be teased out in various ways. Via threads that connect

Venice and Scotland – physical and metaphysical. By drawing: from Giovanni Battista Piranesi, via Robert Adam, John Ruskin / James Whistler and Scarpa, to Le Corbusier. By sensitivity: in both Scarpa + Venice, and Mackintosh / Steven Holl + Glasgow, and their responses to historic environments. By climate: La Serenissima and the Clyde Estuary. Debates like this need to happen in some international context and there is no better than the Venice Biennale.

I think back to the events of the 1980s, chaired by Aldo Rossi and Paolo Portoghesi, in an era when they held them only when there was something important to talk about – with sometimes five years in between. I sense we are there again in the search for material; although the Dutch master-planner, urbanist and architect Rem Koolhaas never fails but to be provocative in the way Rossi was in the 1980s. Always an acute observer of the future in the present, in the OMA room in the Italian Pavilion of the Giardini he suggests in his own polemic:

> 'Embedded in large waves of development there is another kind of transformation at work. The area of the world declared immutable through various regimes of preservation is growing exponentially. At its moment of 'Surreptitious Apotheosis' [pure Koolhaas] preservation does not quite know what to do with its empire. As the scale and importance of preservation escalates each year, the absence of a theory and the lack of interest invested in this seemingly remote domain becomes dangerous. The current moment has almost no idea how to negotiate the co-existence of radical change and radical stasis that is our future.'

It is significant that one of the main images in the OMA room, alongside this quote, was of Damascus just outside the old city walls. The skeleton of a late-1970s megalith, perhaps the victim of the Soviet departure, stands awaiting a use – unlike St Peter's Seminary (also featured by OMA), this never got as far as completion for its intended function, now long forgotten. Yet thirty or so years are but the blink of an eye in the history of Damascus.

Mark Twain wrote on his visit to Damascus in *The Innocents Abroad:*

'She measures time not by days and months and years, but by the empires she has seen rise and crumble to ruin - she is a type of immortality – Damascus has seen all that has ever occurred on earth and still she lives.'

An essential part of this, whether cause or effect, is resilience. Everything is suborned to utility; it can be beautiful but first it must be useful. Everything must be used and used again. Adaptation borne of 5,000 years of experience, a very sophisticated urban model, which may often jar with old-world European sentiments with regards to history, has resulted in a city that works and offers an interesting model on how we might handle our own history. Here, as if in contradiction to Koolhaas' assertions, there has been a negotiation in the co-existence of radical change and radical stasis that has often been that city's 'future'. However, it may also offer paradigms on a theory on 'futures' for preservation. One based on

sound principles of sustainable development and a continual re-use of our existing estate.

Because we have no consistent approach, or theoretical base, anomalies occur. Ours is St Peter's, by Gillespie, Kidd & Coia. Completed in 1966, the building is more interesting as 'ruin' than in its functioning form; not in a French Romantic or Caspar David Friedrich sense, but as an armature for a new take on the building's future. Reconstruction to restoration would be a disaster; a simpler approach is essential. Defining a road map for a future for this unique piece of modern and modernist heritage is key, but given our compliant endeavour to perceive UNESCO and all other heritage bodies as the life blood of our survival in the tourist industry, Rem Koolhaas' plea is all the more urgent.

* Japanese architect Kazuyo Sejima (born 1956) was the curator of the 12th Architecture Biennale in Venice.

# Residues of a Dream World

## Jane Rendell

In *Ursprung des deutschen Trauerspiels* (*The Origin of German Tragic Drama*) conceived of in 1916 and written in 1925, Walter Benjamin discusses *Trauerspiel* (a particular form of baroque theatre based on royal martyr dramas) as a play of sorrow, a ceremonial and ritualised expression of grief, where the hero is both a tyrant and a martyr, sovereign and Christ, part man and part god, grounded in history rather than myth, and emphasising the corporeal as well as the transcendental.[1] In these dramas sadness at the transience of life was represented, for example, as nature petrified in the form of fragments of death, skulls and corpses, and as civilisation disintegrating as ruins of classical monuments and buildings – both were understood as allegories of the human condition. Benjamin stated that 'Allegories are, in the realm of thoughts, what ruins are in the realm of things.'[2]

The figure of the ruin highlights a key aspect of allegory for Benjamin – its relation to time. He notes in baroque allegory 'an appreciation of the transience of things', as well as an expression of sadness about the futility of attempting to save for eternity those things that are transient.[3] Benjamin's study of the baroque also focused on allegorical engravings of the sixteenth century such as Albrecht Dürer's *Melencolia* (1514), in which he describes the 'utensils of active life', as well as tools of creative pursuit 'lying around unused on the floor' next to the figure of melancholy personified, as 'objects of contemplation'.[4] Cultural theorist Susan Buck-Morss has drawn out the importance of the temporal in Benjamin's definition of allegory; how in allegory 'history appears as nature in decay or ruins'.[5]

My first visit to the house I came to call 'Moss Green' had occurred in the spring of 2001. For the next decade I was to walk past Moss Green several times a year, as part of my weekly Sunday walk. In our walks out of Sevenoaks we would sometimes take the route down Oak Lane, then Grassy Lane, past Fig Street, and then along Gracious Lane, drawing to a halt at the fork in the road where Moss Green is situated. When we first saw the house we were entirely enchanted, with the way of life it represented as well as the arresting beauty of its slow yet gentle decay. The house was single-storey, of a brick and timber construction, placed at the top of a scarp slope – with its porch facing a view out over southern England, under which two benches faced one another.

The interior was full of exquisite touches: a perfectly placed built-in cupboard, a carefully detailed windowsill and frame, a thoughtful light switch, a door handle that fitted like a glove. It was hovering at that point where the decay was

An important aspect of the allegorical method is its focus on the image as an 'amorphous fragment' rather than an 'organic totality', producing rather than ambiguity a flexibility of meaning.[6]

still able to provide an atmosphere of charm, where the thought of collapse could be held off, and where it was still possible to imagine oneself into the house, repairing the woodwork and occupying the rooms. But over the years the house has increasingly fallen into disrepair, and our spirits now sink each time we see it. When its slate roof was removed around three years ago the rot really set in and as a structure it is now barely stable. As it slipped past the threshold of being 'save-able', we surrendered our dream of living there ourselves, in a modest rural retreat.

On one visit, years ago, when the house was open to the elements, but some of its contents still present, we noted books on architecture, old journals from the building trade, and piles of photographs. We salvaged a few items – notably one book, *New Architecture of London: A Selection of Buildings since 1930*, along with a selection of black and white photographs, some of which are reproduced here. Recently, in examining the photographs more closely,

Art theorist Peter Bürger has defined Benjamin's understanding of allegory as a four-part schema that involves, first, the isolation of an element as a fragment and the removal of that fragment from its context. Second, the combination of various isolated fragments to create meanings other than those derived from the fragments' original locations. The third important aspect of Benjamin's understanding of allegory for Bürger is his interpretation of the allegorist's activity as melancholic, where the melancholic gaze of the allegorist causes 'life' to be drawn out of the objects she or he assembles. Finally, Bürger considers the viewer's reception of allegory in which history is represented as decline rather than progress.[7]

Benjamin's own major work, the unfinished *Das Passagen-Werk* or *The Arcades Project*, was composed of fragments, including both quotes collected by Benjamin and words written by him between 1927 and 1939. It focused on a particular ruin – the Parisian arcade.[8] Benjamin's specific interest in the Parisian arcades of the early

I have become fascinated with tracking down the buildings imaged in them. As well as the architectural qualities of the structures, I have had five text-based clues to work with – a board in front of one block of flats with the name 'Ernest Knifton Ltd.'; a car parked outside another with the registration plate 'SLX 956'; a street sign reading 'Westmoreland Terrace'; and letters over the entrances to two other buildings with the words '1-24 Edmund Street' and 'Witl-'.

I have managed to track down most of the structures – it turns out that the majority we now regard as modernist icons, such as The Elmington Estate (1957), Picton Street, London SE5, designed by the LCC Architect's Dept., now largely demolished; The Hallfield Estate (1952–1955), Bishops Bridge Road, W2, designed by Tecton, Drake and Lasdun for Paddington Borough Council; The Alton East Estate (1952–1955), Portsmouth Road, SW15, designed by the LCC Architect's Dept.; The Alton West Estate

nineteenth century, along with certain material fragments associated with them, for example dust and mannequins, concerned their role as dialectical images.[9] According to Benjamin, as thesis the arcades 'flower'; they are palaces of commodity consumption and the wish-images of the dreaming collective of the early nineteenth century. As antithesis, in the early twentieth century, the arcades are in decline; they are ruins, no longer desired by the consuming populace.[10] In his own words: 'They are residues of a dream-world …'[11]

As a particular form of dialectical synthesis, the arcade is a dialectical image – a moment where the past is recognised in the present as a ruin that was once desired. Benjamin's image captures dialectical contradiction in an instant: 'The dialectic, in standing still, makes an image.'[12]

(1955–1959), Roehampton Lane, SW15, designed by the LCC Architect's Dept.; and Churchill Gardens (1950–1962), Grosvenor Road, Lupus Street, SW1, designed by Powell and Moya for Westminster City Council.

What has happened today to the socialist ideals of modernism? Some of the modern movement's public housing projects have become oases of cool property in the London postcodes associated with the rich, well-maintained, sometimes privatised and provided with concierge schemes, while in poorer neighbourhoods they have been allowed to decline materially, often not included in 'major works' programmes – the large-scale council repair and maintenance cycles. In aspiring regeneration zones, some have been demolished because the original construction is viewed to be too expensive to overhaul, others are in ruins, or at least the years of neglect have led to conditions of terminal dereliction. But the seeming pragmatic solution offered by viewing the problem as an

The ruin that features in baroque dramas in terms of decay and disintegration, and as a site for a melancholic reflection on the transience of human and material existence, becomes politically instructive as a dialectical image in *Das Passagen-Werk*.

economic concern, is a symptom of an underlying problem where modern architecture is itself seen as the cause of the malaise, intimately tied through its Brutalist aesthetic to deterministic design and social deprivation. This has forced the designers of certain regeneration schemes, the Elmington Estate for one, to adopt a new architectural language: one not so obviously 'modern' and therefore capable of suggesting better standards of living in a less utopian manner.

Returning to Moss Green once again, several weekends ago, much of the timberwork had collapsed and was lying in pieces across the grass. I turned one rotten section over to reveal two words painted in fast fragmenting white letters: 'May Morn'. This, I remembered, was the building's name plaque, which had been located at the entrance to the plot, framed by brambles, when we first came across the house.

For Benjamin, a key quality of the dialectical image is its ability to create a moment when the usual patterns of thinking stop and new ones are given the chance to emerge: 'Where thinking suddenly stops in a configuration pregnant with tensions, it gives that configuration a shock.'[13] Montage was for him a progressive form because it had the ability to 'interrupt the context into which it is inserted'.[14] A technique he admired in other artworks, Benjamin used montage as a form of textual construction in his own *Das Passagen-Werk*: 'Method of this project: literary montage. I needn't *say* anything. Merely show ... The first stage in this undertaking will be to carry over the principle of montage into history. That is, to assemble large-scale constructions out of the smallest and most precisely cut components. Indeed to discover in the analysis of the small individual moment "the crystal of the total event".'[15]

1 George Steiner, 'Introduction', in Walter Benjamin, *The Origin of German Tragic Drama* [1925], trans. John Osborne (London: Verso, 1977) pp. 16-8.
2 Benjamin, *The Origin of German Tragic Drama*, p. 178.
3 Ibid, p. 223.
4 Ibid, p. 140.
5 Susan Buck-Morss, *The Dialectics of Seeing: Walter Benjamin and the Arcades Project* (Cambridge, MA: MIT Press, 1991) pp. 166–8.
6 Benjamin, *The Origin of German Tragic Drama*, pp. 176–7.
7 Peter Bürger, *Theory of the Avant-Garde* (Minneapolis: University of Minnesota Press, 1984) p. 69.
8 Walter Benjamin, *The Arcades Project (1927–39)*, trans. Howard Eiland and Kevin McLaughlin (Cambridge, MA: Harvard University Press, 1999).
9 Rolf Tiedemann, 'Dialectics at a Standstill: Approaches to the *Passagen-werk*', Benjamin, *The Arcades Project*, p. 932.
10 Walter Benjamin, 'Materials for the Exposé of 1935', *The Arcades Project*, p. 910.
11 Walter Benjamin, 'Paris: The Capital of the Nineteenth Century' [1935], trans. Quintin Hoare, *Charles Baudelaire: A Lyric Poet in the Era of High Capitalism*, trans. Harry Zohn (London: New Left Books, 1997) p. 176.
12 Benjamin, 'Materials for the Exposé of 1935', p. 911.
13 Walter Benjamin, 'Theses on the Philosophy of History' [1940], trans. Harry Zohn, *Illuminations* (London: Fontana, 1992) pp. 245–55, p. 254.
14 Buck-Morss, pp. 67 and 77.
15 Benjamin, *The Arcades Project*, pp. 460–1.

Morn and mourn are homonyms. One suggests a beginning, the other an ending. Due to their deteriorating material states, the 'Moss Green' house, the paper of the photographs, and the painted letters 'May Morn' all point towards their own disintegration – or endings – yet the buildings contained within the photographs are shown at the beginning of their life. What does it mean to turn back now and examine these ruins – these deteriorating photographs of modernist icons – at an early moment – a spring-time?

Note: This image-text piece is composed of two strands. The text on the right, positioned in between colour images taken by myself, of the ruined house – May Morn – built in the Arts & Crafts style is set in Golden type, a font designed by William Morris in 1890. The text on the left is set in Helvetica, a modern sans-serif typeface developed by Swiss typeface designer Max Miedinger with Eduard Hoffmann in 1957, the same year as the Elmington Estate, one of the housing estates depicted in the black and white photographs found at May Morn, was built. This work draws on previous research on dialectical images in the writings of Walter Benjamin published in Jane Rendell, *Art and Architecture* (London: IB Tauris, 2006) and a longer image-text work, 'May Morn', published in Gareth Evans and Di Robson (eds.), *Towards The Re-Enchantment: Place and Its Meanings* (London: Artevents, 2010), pp. 40–59.

# Conservation and Preservation

The following quotes are excerpts from the debate in Venice that took place on 21 November 2010. The same applies to the excerpts on pages 58-61, and 82-7.

It is no coincidence that you have a Biennale about modern architecture in Venice, because there isn't any here. People went to Rome in the eighteenth century to look at ruins, I suppose because they tell you about what happens over time, or they're illustrations of what happens to things over time. A ruin is a way of concretising one's thought about something, a thought instrument.

*Edward Hollis*

If you accept that a functional aspect of the building is gone, then it can be a landscape, and the landscape and building just merge into one. Then it is about some practical things: about opening up access, making paths, making connections to the whole community. That discussion then makes it more interesting about how different layers of ideas could be introduced.

*Ian Gilzean*

It's a relatively new proposition to make any attempt to save a post-war modernist building. Something that really struck me was the idea that post-war restoration is like a black hole, in terms of preservation. So we can imagine that in two or three hundred years, people will look back and from 1940 to 1980, there won't be anything there, because we won't have kept it, as we won't have valued it. Because the social ideology that made it is seen to be bankrupt, so we collectively erase this piece of history. It's based on the idea that those in power simply didn't like it, or can't come to terms with the political failure that led to those commissions being realised, rather than seeing it as an incredible period of social history.

*Angus Farquhar*

Watching it I thought that in a way the movie [Murray Grigor's *Space and Light* and *Space and Light Revisited*] could be the conservation of the building. The building is now preserved in film, practically in its original state, and in its found state, as a ruin. To be a wee bit argumentative, why not let it be?

*Henry McKeown*

We could be accused of being very nostalgic about this building, because of the firm that built it and the characters who were architects. There is a sense to a degree that these guys should be revered, because we were taught by them and they were the last of their generation. But, where do you begin to establish a value of a ruin? We talk about it as a ruin: there was no war, there was no conquest, no bombs dropped on it, or, like in Rome or other civilisations, where the architecture of ruin is a consequence of certain major and dramatic events. Therefore the importance of that as a record of history becomes far, far more important, just for argument's sake, than, say, St Peter's. Doing a bit of Ruskin Wikipedia, he says that the building's age is the most important aspect of its preservation, and I wonder what he meant by that. What age does a building have to be before you can begin to think of it as 'well, it is a ruin'? Is it important, does it have a value in terms of the cultural history of a place?

*Henry McKeown*

The idea of conserving a ruin is very interesting. I don't think a dramatic event has to have taken place to make it interesting. The vast majority of buildings that we preserve throughout the world have fallen into ruin. They generally go through a period of neglect, often hundreds of years of neglect. Then we begin to see the cultural value as historical objects, then we begin to think about saving them, and this is what Ruskin was arguing for: for the authenticity of the ruin as well as the authenticity of the living building. But as soon as you mention conservation, it is very difficult to make that an absurdity, to say: well, when do you stop, when do you start, what is a ruin, when is the end of time for historical monuments? Once you have decided, as a society, as a culture, that this thing needs saving, this thing needs preserving in some form or another, then you work out practically how to do that. We have to think about that when we are dealing with St Peter's as a ruin.

*Ranald MacInnes*

We look back at it [St Peter's] with slightly rose-tinted spectacles, because we all like mid-century modernism now. But you have to remember that it was one of the most reviled styles on earth in the 1980s and 1990s. There may have been many reasons why the building didn't survive and is no longer used as it was intended, but I suspect one of them was that people didn't like it, they didn't celebrate it. So it died this extraordinarily quick death while there are plenty of equivalent buildings that have survived and been re-understood and re-valued now. I remember the Trellick Tower being derided in the 1970s and 1980s, and the Barbican, and now they're massively celebrated, as are Le Corbusier's tower blocks. So thinking about what the nature of involvement can be in the space, the question is: how will the place engage?

*Adam Sutherland*

Whether we should be nostalgic about it: I don't actually see that that is a problem. Why not? That can be a driving force for how we respond to it, and I think that is something you can build on.

*Ian Gilzean*

The real reason [for the Church's withdrawal of seminary use] probably was the fact that it was uneconomic to run the building. So I think it's unfair to say that it was an unhappy place. A lot of students didn't like certain aspects of it because they would have preferred to have a swimming pool etc, but a lot of them loved walking in the grounds and the sharing of Mass twice a day..

*Murray Grigor*

I'm glad we can't just go and create some instant fix for St Peter's, because as a result, we can't make the wrong decisions. We have to do this slowly: we have to do it respecting the inherent dignity that is actually transcending the ruin, and slowly bring it back. We can make the right decisions by not being able to make the wrong ones by moving forward too fast. That's our start.

*Angus Farquhar*

My fear [for Kilmahew / St Peter's] is that there'd be signs everywhere saying 'don't do this', 'don't do that', 'watch this step', 'watch that step'... I'm probably premature, but this project could go a long way in challenging some of these preconceptions about health and safety, because it dominates everything we do.

*Alan Pert*

The very challenges of the building are the things that create the opportunities, in the sense that conservation practice would normally say, 'Let's look for an end use', and once you had found the end use, the ability to develop, the ability to raise money would all pour in. There is a sense of this building waiting for a purpose that is never going to arrive. There is no commercial solution, no practical solution for it, and it will sit and wait forever unless something is done.

*David Cook*

It is a very strong cultural artefact, whatever you think about its condition and whatever might happen. The idea of the humble approach and just investing some time and thought and careful consideration is a very appropriate way to move it forward, because there is a huge potential there.

*Ian Gilzean*

One of the things that seems to be coming through quite strongly is a sort of dichotomy between the landscape being important and the building ... The ruin is there, it just happens to be in a landscape, and we all think it is much more important now than actually the building originally was. If we start to look at the building and its restoration and preservation, then it is taking us back to the whole debate about how to deal with that as a subject.
It is an interesting dichotomy, the whole idea of making it a landscape project rather than an architecture project. But I also worry: if we then re-focus it on the building, are we then ending up with a position of almost atrophy, with a building there that is so sensitive ... Is that a situation in which you actually have something that is so loaded in terms of memory, or in terms of its own presence, that you can't do anything to it, that you freeze?

*Gordon Murray*

# Anxious Care and Unsightly Aids
## Edward Hollis

Once upon a time, an architecture student broke into an abandoned seminary. He pulled a piece of timber from the wall, and took it away with him. He made it into a shelf, put it by his drawing board, and sat down with it to wait for his tutor. The tutor didn't notice the bookshelf, and my friend wasn't going to point it out to him. You see: the tutor had designed the seminary. Perched on a stool between the master and a stolen fragment of the masterpiece, the student – vandal, relic hunter, secret admirer – felt keenly the ironies of his position.

The seminary, St Peter's in Cardross, was abandoned in 1984, and has since acquired a mythical status among artists and architects. Once a modernist phalanstery, the work of the prominent practice Gillespie, Kidd & Coia, St Peter's is now a chapel perilously hidden in an enchanted forest, a Piranesian ruin, and the wreck of scheme after scheme for redevelopment. But ruination is a process of entropy, not a steady state: if nothing happens St Peter's will soon melt away, reduced by theft, arson, rhododendrons and rain.

Outside the student's window was another masterpiece in crisis. Charles Rennie Mackintosh's Glasgow School of Art was built as an art school, but it's become an icon, and the requirements of the two don't match. Art is a messy, toxic, noisy business – one ill suited to guided tours and the contemplation of the connoisseur; and while St Peter's may be subject to the laws of entropy, the Art School is falling prey to atrophy. Soon enough it'll have to be turned into a museum.

Entropy and Atrophy are the traps into which every building will eventually fall; and Venice has been sinking into both of them for some time. Venice, wrote John Ruskin in 1851:

> 'is still left for our beholding in the final period of her decline, a ghost upon the sands of the sea, so weak – so quiet – so bereft of her loveliness that we might well doubt, as we watched her faint reflection in the mirage of the lagoon, which was the city and which the shadow.'
>
> (*The Stones of Venice: The Foundations*, London, 1851)

*The Stones of Venice* was written to halt that decline. In *The Seven Lamps of Architecture* he stated:

'Watch an old building with an anxious care; guard it as best you may, and at any cost, from every influence of dilapidation ... bind it together with iron where it loosens; stay it with timber where it declines; do not care about the unsightliness of the aid.' ('Memory', *The Seven Lamps of Architecture*, London, 1849)

Ruskin was all too influential. The eleven million tourists who visit Venice every year find themselves in a heritage experience surpassed only by the simulated Venices of Vegas and Macao. It is ironic that the Biennale, that celebration of all that is new in art and architecture, takes place in a city made to appear as if time stood still.

Conservation is an attempt to stop time in its tracks; but buildings are always changing: if they don't, they are ready for the wrecking ball or the glass case. We build buildings to last, and when they do, they outlive the people who made them and the purposes for which they were made. Freed of the insubstantial pageants that made them, they must be altered to suit altered needs in altered worlds. It will happen again, and again.

It's an uncomfortable position. Change is unpredictable, and always has been: architects might hope to predict what happens to their creations in the short term, but in the *longue durée* no one knows what will happen. Architectural intentions are like the first limb of an exquisite corpse: incomplete, contingent, and pregnant with possibility.

We have to work with the unpredictable, and Ruskin knew it. His plea might have begun with 'anxious care', but it ends with the curious injunction: 'do not care about the unsightliness of the aid.' It's a provocative challenge – no one wants to make something ugly – because it suggests that no building is ever complete. The unsightly aid is a problem postponed until later: it is an admission that further work will be required. Perhaps, one day, the aid itself will be watched over with anxious care,

and be propped up by another, even more unsightly one. Think, for example, of the celebrated so-called chicken run at the top of Mackintosh's art school – it was an 'unsightly aid' once, necessitated by the expansion of the building; now it's an iconic piece of architecture.

It's an idea with a pedigree in Venice itself. In the 1960s the architect Carlo Scarpa dealt with atrophied monuments by superimposing modernist fragments – unsightly aids of his own devising – onto their classical carcasses. We are left free to inhabit and roam the space in between the two without having to commit to either. One day, perhaps, someone else will add fragments of their own to Scarpa's collages of past and present.

But the pedigree is much older than that. Venice was founded when the citizens of Roman Aquileia faced barbarian attack. They knew they wouldn't be able to keep their venerable buildings the way they were. Like the architecture student, they ripped them to pieces and floated them out into the lagoon. They bound the fragments together with iron and stayed them with timber, and they are still there. The city was only ever an unsightly aid, an altered state, obliged to alter again, or, if not, to become a shadow on the mirage of a lagoon.

The unsightly aid is a process, not a product. The wreckage of plan after grand plan for St Peter's proves that ruins will not be resurrected overnight. On the table at present, NVA's plans for the ruined seminary and woodlands are not plans in the conventional sense, but rather the initiation of an incremental process that begins with small moves: a walk, a productive garden, and perhaps, one day soon, acquisition and the start of a new life for a building. This creative progression, initiated by NVA and maintained by the people who live around the site, is iterative. The site provokes a reaction (walking for example), which is imposed back onto the site (as a path), which, altered, provokes an altered reaction (a destination for the path), and so on. In Glasgow, Steven Holl's new building is, unlike Mackintosh's, filled with spaces whose function is unassigned and indeterminate, in the hope that generations of students and staff will make of them what they will.

Goethe wrote that architecture is frozen music; but experience teaches us that it just plays very slowly. It is pointless to dictate what the buildings of the future will look like, or how they will work – we aren't prophets - but we can both trace and steer their evolution in the here and now.

# Wider Landscape

We have talked a lot about the building. The landscape is coming across almost as an adjunct, a sideline, but actually the focus of the current proposals has always been the building within the landscape; not just trying to save the building, but to look at the landscape and find solutions that emerge out of that.

*David Cook*

Now that the seminary as an institution has dissolved and the building itself has dissolved, can we think about a landscape that might potentially kind of re-open? There is a whole different way of telling this story and opening up this kind of utopian moment.

*Moira Jeffrey*

Landscape tends to get talked about in terms of being this sort of benign thing. It is just there with its own gradual little processes. With this situation it is almost a reversal of those positions: talking about the building for which there is no defined function, essentially bringing the functions to the landscape. That has a much broader, social, cultural context, particularly in West-central Scotland at this point in time.

*Rolf Roscher*

The idea that all these enclosures, and particularly the nuns' enclosures, aren't enclosures any more is incredible. André Breton made this surrealist suggestion for monuments in Paris that you surround them with walls and nobody should ever visit them, and that you should just imagine them. The notion about breaking down an institution ... and the literal breaking down of the walls and the landscape flowing sideways through a building that was linear in the other direction, actually begins to really open up that enclosure and allow people to occupy it, maybe with garden sheds ... It doesn't have to be 'here's the grand plan'.

*Edward Hollis*

What also comes across in Murray Grigor's film is the drama, or the dramatic potential of the site, of the landscape, of the building itself and the relationship between all of these. And to somehow exploit that, but do it in such a way that involves the local community, the people of Scotland, and also the international community.

*Ian Gilzean*

St Peter's offers an opportunity to prototype and explore the idea of a new productive landscape. That is about function. That is about people engaging with it in different ways. Currently there are no examples of that. It is a very specific approach within the idea of productivity, of doing things, of people engaging, and it goes back to that point about de-institutionalisation, and about an independent, individual, creative learning.

*Rolf Roscher*

You encounter St Peter's through this kind of patrilineal handing down of the story of St Peter's: a wonderful, but hierarchical kind of teaching narrative, the way in which it is transmitted, and the way in which it has been received within a kind of revival of utopian modernism and notions of the failures of modernism. The space and the landscape itself are very, very challenging to encounter. I simply don't go to St Peter's because this language of going to a ruined, locked up, dangerous landscape is not something that I, as a woman, or a parent of young children, would consider. It is a male narrative for me, this kind of 'going and having an adventure'.

*Moira Jeffrey*

The modern movement in architecture was dependent on institutions. The ideas that we are exploring are about taking St Peter's as a ruin of a particular thing, and then re-investigating not just the building, but the landscape, the whole thing, as an exploration of how you devolve creative decision-making to people. To bring a lot of individual, smaller decisions to something that was, by its very nature, one big decision, one big move, is a core topic at this moment in time.

*Rolf Roscher*

I think that one of the beauties of St Peter's is the premise that landscape is tension. So many of the comments that have come through in conversation so far actually expose that early idea of tension, but it is a very productive tension.

*Hayden Lorimer*

We should maybe overcome the notion of building and think of it as a landscape, as a structure. Try to integrate the local people, through for instance making these paths and having picnics, and these paths should be extended. That is about use, because we are not doing anything else in landscape. We [landscape architects] want to make things visible in the landscape when we design a park or a garden, or if we do a little intervention somewhere. We try to make the path as intelligent as possible so that people's imagination is going to be grasped, and they are animated to re-think an area.

*Tilman Latz*

Duisberg-Nord in the Ruhr area is absolutely inspirational. It's done with incredible invention - putting living lilies into open furnaces, plunge pools into water tanks and operas in the middle of a Bessemer converter. That would have been a wonderful way of keeping some of the great things of our whole industrial heritage alive.

*Murray Grigor*

Another term that is really quite powerful is one that the anthropologist Tim Ingold has used, which is to conceive of landscape as a taskscape, as something that is formed out of the continuity of practice as it evolves through it. So to begin to think from present to future, to conceive of St Peter's as a taskscape, as something that actually begins to be inhabited, something that is dwelt in, something that people spend time doing things in, actually creates a different type of scape. It's that scaping project that is the fascinating one.

*Hayden Lorimer*

# Once Upon a Time ...
## Tilman Latz

I remember driving with my family through northern Italy as a child, and, somewhere between Bolzano and Verona, passing an old castle ruin that was embedded in the rocks high above the valley. Suddenly my brother and I were driven by an unconscious awareness of the importance of this place. We mobilised all available forces to stir our parents into action and to turn the car towards these 'old useless stones'. Since little kids can be very insistent, it was not surprising that the struggle ended with a full victory for the younger generation. Shortly after we discovered this miraculous place: the remains of massive walls and the holes for some former ceiling constructions. How had it functioned? Was it a specific defence mechanism?

Swept away by our fantasies, my brother and I dreamt of robbing knights blocking the gorge to keep powerful enemies away from their possessions. In our imagination, they looked like our little colourful plastic toys. Fierce fighting led to victory, prisoners were taken and the triumphant combatants returned to their damsels, singing and joking on their beautiful horses.

We tried to clamber around the place, shocking our parents when making it to the top of some old constructions that were far too high for little kids. The castle's potential main tower gave us a perfect panoramic view. We speculated on how the medieval knights would have observed every movement in the valley.

These memories stimulated our thoughts for quite a while. Back home we constructed our own castles from Lego and cardboard, re-enacted speculative court scenes, discussed how the castle must have been properly fortified and analysed its setting in the landscape, read countless books about the times of the knights and consequently simulated history as it might have been.

From an abstract point of view, the inherent importance of the physical remains transcended into our lives. It enriched our imagination with stories, which had never really happened before. Each little detail of the ruins, which might have been caused by weathering or other incidents in time, created another drama and effectively kept stirring

our memory. Backed up by our acquired historical knowledge, everything transformed nearly into reality.

These are the fabric real ruins are made of. They are part of a much broader mental landscape, which goes beyond what can actually be seen – a multilayered experience. They stimulate our imagination, offer an environment enriched with playful details and meaning, and a place of opportunity – all of a sudden they become alive …

Our parents were generally taken by ruins too, but their imagination was already broadly satisfied by just seeing them from afar. To say it in a theoretician's language: in general adults' early memories and their actual reality mix up with acquired knowledge, and a multilayered individual experience is generated. 'Some old useless stones', if strictly observed through the eyes of a technician, were able to create a new perception.

The sculptures in Bomarzo's Bosco dei Mostri (Monsters' Grove) by Pier Francesco Orsini (1528–1588) function in exactly the same way as those old castle ruins did for my brother and I. Certainly astonishing, as they are referred to in many descriptions, the abundant collection of monsters, almost collapsing houses (see p. 83) and fighting scenes of ancient gods seem to mock the fears of the people of Renaissance Italy. Visitors can use the objects for picnics, parties and inspiring conversations, allowing different approaches to their surroundings. The garden broke with the traditional iconographic positioning of sculptures and other garden pieces. Orsini replaced it with an additional intuitive, bodily experience and a sense of individual adventure. The result was consequently much more evocative, full of implied narrative.

Much later the use of architecture, sculptures and ruins had reached a level of perfection within the English garden tradition, where they were not only used to organise and orientate the various green spaces; they were clearly meant to stimulate visions of a presumably glorious past as an ideal for the present and the future. The sophisticated arrangements of little artistic interventions gave the visitor a wealth of possible narratives, each object offering enough material for the content of a thick book.

## A Storyteller and a Timeless Marvel

In modern civilisation we tend to try and solve problems immediately. For St Peter's this would mean seeing a structure and recognising that it is threatened by the continuous assaults of weathering and decay. Consequently we would develop scenarios for how to save it and propose different phasing strategies. The decision of what to do is then bound to three questions: can we afford it? What are we going to use it for? And, who is going to maintain it? Very often business plans then decide about the destiny of such structures in a very short period of time. We look for immediate salvation – a hotel and conference centre, an adventure park, an outdoor-sports centre ... just to mention some of the most typical responses to such sites in the recent past.

But what is needed is an innovative conception and adaptive approach. We do need to think about what St Peter's was and what it is today. That is a discussion about values and collective memory: about whether we're seeing such an object as a collective obligation and public place, or as something we can hand over for other types of redevelopment. Finally it is about what it means to us now and what it could mean to us in the future.

St Peter's Seminary and its surrounding landscape, as they stand now, are artefacts that convey the narrative of a place with a high potential for individual enrichment and even excessive imagination, simply because they are unique ruins.

What is striking about them is that over the last thirty years they have developed into a mythical entropic wreck. They are neither authentically restored, nor deformed through inappropriate functions. The remains are pure symbols of a very specific period in architectural history, of an optimistic and relatively modern epoch in religious development, which comprises countless stories simultaneously. These are tales of caducity and the power of nature, of myths of superstition and ingenious inventions, attraction and mischief – embedded in a miraculous modern temple. This unique quality could easily be lost if a conventional conservation approach were applied.

If we can find a kind of new interpretation, a new 'narrative of St Peter's', we might be able not to talk about one specific function, but to open it up for many different ones and to occupy that space and reuse it. And we might also find a new interpretation of the whole landscape, so that it can metamorphose in a certain sense into new functions.

I think we need an approach that leads to a practical application in time and in accordance with the public interests. But it is equally important to respect the notion of time that is now accumulated within the site. Consequently it is just as important to take time for interventions, to keep things open and propose structures that can develop further and take new ideas on board. This could include the thoughts and ideas of local people. That's what makes such a project sustainable over time.

Originally the architects of St Peter's were challenged to find a non-dogmatic new architectural form, which created on the one hand a 'sacred place', and on the other hand respected and transformed ecclesiastical traditions of a thousand years of the Roman Catholic Church in Scotland into a conceptual and spatial programme. By cleaning and restoring it, the seminary could possibly tell this story, but it would be devoid of any of its own further history. It would be just another clean museum piece.

## A Landscape

With the project Landschaftspark Duisburg-Nord (1990–2000), Latz + Partner has gathered experiences with these types of complex spatial structures, left over after (industrial) activity has ceased. It is a 230-hectare brownfield site, with three blast furnaces and their massive technical installations, full of railroads, dams, ore and coal bunkers, water purification channels, cooling towers, cast iron and steel manufacturing areas, chemical facilities, power generation halls and distribution centres. Leftovers of a glorious past, simply abandoned and now exposed to natural processes, the industrial fabric has become a substrate for pioneer plants and animals – an archaeological and ecological treasure trove.

In the design process we decided to let all these elements tell their own stories, to keep most of the structures and to give them their time before we intervened. We learnt that it is helpful to re-think the area and come up with a new interpretation of the structures before we talk about functions. In this case:

1 We interpreted the industrial machinery as an outstanding landscape, and
2 We transformed the material and spaces in such a way that they became perceivable as landscape, meant for others, by
   a Giving access and allowing all kinds of activities;
   b Celebrating the 'nature' of the site in all its aspects;
   c Adding specific programmes to foster human activity and symbolise change.

That also meant penetrating, opening up and transforming some of the structures as well as morphing them into an existing language of materials (hard and soft) in order to allow for an integrative and sustainable approach.

Rather than looking at what St Peter's was, we could look at what it has actually become: curious visitors have traced new pathways and picnic areas in the grounds that lead towards the seminary. Architectural elements have fallen down, thus creating new spatial contexts. Remnants of much older architecture and gardens punctuate the terrain. In the natural process of decay, animals and vegetation have taken over the buildings …

By initially giving access to people to get into the buildings or defining limited interventions such as secure pathways, vistas and possibilities to enjoy the changing nature, the structure becomes interesting. Like paths on a special mountain, these limited interventions could save it from further decay in one area, opening up possibilities of accessibility and active use in others. Accessibility seems the key factor to allow people to get inspired, animate their imagination and charge the spaces with new stories. We could possibly say: 'we need to re-conquer, reclaim and re-activate that powerful landscape for the people.' Is this a romantic and therefore unrealistic vision?

Claude Lorrain (1600–1682) painted romantic interpretations and idealisations of 'Nature'. His work laid the foundation for the notion of romantic landscapes as willingly constructed carriers of meaning, which later inspired numerous garden and park designers all around Europe. Since ancient times mankind has re-used given structures to make economic use of existing structures and materials. In doing so it has literally incorporated the glorious memories of its ancestors, their achievements and their power. Things might look romantic from today's point of view, but in reality they are the outcomes of a rational thinking process. The destruction of a culture and erasure of reminders has happened over time, when we wanted to get rid of undesired meanings, symbols and values. But do we want to forget St Peter's, its outstanding architectural importance and history?

One proposition during the Venice debate was to interpret the building of St Peter's as a landscape. Following this idea, we should maybe overcome the notion of building, as this always asks for function. We could rather think of it as a landscape, an open system that can transform over time and assimilate as many functions and interpretations as possible. Then a strategy of a 'controlled decay and growth' is maybe applicable.

We could think of it as a structure which integrates the local people and their interests. And we could also intervene with new ideas for attractions, making use of existing structures and processes for new purposes: rainwater, endemic and pioneer plants, light and shadow ...

# Institutionalised Landscape
## Rolf Roscher

It's not just any ruin. It's a particular kind of ruin at a particular point in time.

The Japanese Pavilion at the Venice Architecture Biennale examined how cities have evolved and the institutions that deliver particular forms of buildings and public space. The proposition explored how you move beyond institutional models to the idea of the regenerative city that's made up of a lot of small, individual decisions.

That's why St Peter's and its state of ruin is so relevant. It's a building that could only have existed in the context of a big institution and at a certain point in time. In terms of its specific form, the modern movement in architecture was dependent on institution.

The ideas that we're developing are about taking St Peter's as an institutional ruin and re-investigating not just the building but the landscape, in totality, as a locus to explore how you devolve creative decision-making to people; to bring a lot of individual smaller decisions to something that was, by its nature, one big decision, one big move.

The starting point has always been thinking about the need to find a function for the building. The building has to have a function. Landscape tends to get talked about in terms of being this benign 'thing'. It is just there with its own gradual little processes.

In some ways the plan for St Peter's is almost a reversal of those positions, where there is a less defined function for the building, and the emphasis is on bringing more of the functions to the wider landscape. The landscape is the generator of activity and change.

If you have a 'romantic' landscape setting (like the Victorian designed landscape setting of St Peter's), at best you stroll through it, you look at it and you enjoy it in those terms. The core question is: what is a twenty-first-century public landscape for the kind of society that we now are? What do we need it to do?

It needs to be an active, creative and productive landscape. It needs to be peopled. That is important socially and culturally for Scotland at this moment.

*You look around the urban conurbation that is greater Glasgow, the peripheral estates and so on; there are thousands of hectares of essentially dysfunctional landscape. It does nothing for communities; people can't engage with it, it is locked in an unusable state. It is institutionalised and dysfunctional land. It has disengaged generations of people from landscape, from physical activity, from ideas of local diet, where their food comes from, from all of these things, profound social problems.*

The following essay is an expansion of the above statements made during the Kilmahew / St Peter's debate at the Venice Biennale.

My point of reference for considering issues of institution and their particular relevance to St Peter's Seminary lie in the writings of Ivan Illich (1926–2002, an Austrian philosopher, Roman Catholic priest and social critic) – specifically the essays and lectures in the publication *The Rivers North of the Future*.* Through the various texts in this collection, ideas of institution, religion and modernity are explored and their inter-relationship discussed.

Illich begins by considering the custom in early Christian households of having 'an extra mattress, a bit of candle, and some dry bread in case the Lord Jesus should knock at the door in the form of a stranger without a roof'. He observes that this act became subject to institutionalisation after the Christian Church achieved official status within the Roman Empire. Special houses were established, financed by the community, which were charged with taking care of people without a home. Illich argues that what had been a 'truly free choice' became an 'institutionalisation of neighbourliness'. Although this is an attempt to 'extend Christian hospitality', he argues that it immediately perverts it. He develops this point further and his overarching argument is perhaps best summarised in the collective heading for the essays: 'the corruption of the best is the worst'.

Illich notes that the power to transform this 'giving freely of oneself' is first claimed by 'the Church and later by the many secular institutions stamped from its mould. Wherever I look for the roots

of modernity, I find them in the attempts of the churches to institutionalise, legitimise, and manage Christian vocation'.

This broad argument connecting and tracing the inter-relationship of the Church, the institutionalisation of ideals and modernity is very instructive in understanding the resonance of the ruined St Peter's Seminary. Considered in this historical context, the ruined building becomes a powerful physical manifestation of these ideas. It reveals something profound about the development and form of our society. It is not just a story about a piece of architecture from a few decades ago – it demonstrates something that has taken shape over a much longer period of time.

The ruined building and the propositions being developed for the site also signal a wider (international) cultural position specific to our times. At the start of the twenty-first century many societies are beginning to question and reframe previous assumptions. The optimism and utopian

ideal founded on 'technological modernity' is shown to unquestionably have its shortcomings and limitations (not least of which are the increasingly clear environmental thresholds and the consequently clear time-limited nature of this construct). This raises many difficult questions and challenges, among them: what do you do with the architectural and infrastructural artefacts of the era of institutional modernity?

Themes we have been exploring and discussing in relation to St Peter's were woven through many of the more interesting exhibits in the Venice Biennale: critiques of modernism, critiques of embedded values in conservation, utopian visions of new communities closely tied to productive landscapes and so on.

'Tokyo Metabolising' in the Japanese Pavilion considered the different urban forms that arise from 'monarchist' and 'capitalist' cities and explored the notion of the city regenerating through the dynamism of the urban village – the city regenerated

through many small individual decisions with 'daily life at its core'. To consider the propositions in terms of Illich's observations on religion, institution and modernity: it is not a Christian society, but predominantly Shinto / Buddhist, the form of the urban village is not institutionally directed and its origins are arguably 'pre-modern'.

Here the dwellings incorporate transitional space where strangers can enter the essentially 'private' realm. The forms encourage the use of outdoor space – the 'interstices' become usable and green. These could be interpreted as a physical manifestation of 'non-institutional neighbourliness' – arguably equivalent to the early Christian custom of open welcome that Illich describes.

The evolution and short lifespan of the St Peter's Seminary buildings is fascinating considered in the light of Illich's argument. Built by the Archdiocese as a seminary in an isolated location distinct from the local community, the nature of both its origin and functioning are 'institutional'. The form of

architecture – the modernist 'mega-structure' – is dependent upon this institutional origin and twentieth-century construction technology. One of the reasons for the building's short lifespan as an operational seminary was the Church's change in approach to training priests. Rather than isolating them from society, trainee priests were brought into the communities that they might serve: if not full de-institutionalisation, then certainly a step in that direction. In this respect, the current propositions for the site could be seen as the next step in a process started by the Church in the 1970s.

The ideas manifest in the ruined seminary buildings make this a unique place to explore the role of public space at the start of the twenty-first century. The project offers a unique tension: to explore ideas of a 'metabolising' creative and productive landscape within the context of an iconic modern, institutional ruin.

* Ivan Illich, *The Rivers North of the Future – The Testament of Ivan Illich as told to David Cayley* (Toronto: House of Anansi Press, 2005)

# Wider Landscape

Local residents have offered their thoughts and opinions about the Kilmahew / St Peter's site, and its future. Here is a selection (see also pages 96-7).

We enjoy the stunning architecture of the college and the beautiful woodlands that surround it.

Over the last ten years, the woodland has really deteriorated. It needs a level of woodland management.

The young are interested in growing but don't know how. If they can go to learn and grow with others – as a supported activity, it would be a good local activity.

Keep the walled garden special – allotments should be elsewhere.

The site has a sense that you can always discover something new. It has a sense of mystery.

The gradual deterioration of the grounds is sad to witness now that it is so heavily overgrown.

I enjoy the wildness of the grounds and woods, the river, walled garden and the original house before it burned down.

It would be good to have foresting courses for local people.

That's what gives it a local flavour: the local people who have worked on the land.

I like the wild unspoilt nature of the grounds without formality or signs. It's a place of discovery in an age of spoon-fed recreation.

I enjoy a feeling of wilderness, yet so close to the local community. Good for viewing wildlife.

# The Keys to the Kingdom
## Hayden Lorimer

### Many St Peter's

The figure stands alone, elevated on a simple stone pediment. Hewn from granite, his pose is one of peaceful rectitude, hands held out, clasped in prayer. St Peter seems entirely oblivious to the traffic only twelve paces distant, rumbling away to the city limits or channelled towards its centre. He has been weathered by northerly climes, is shaded from direct sunlight by neighbouring buildings, and an overhanging lime tree. No wonder then that his shoulders and the lower sweep of his vestments are hued a matching green. Dirtying my fingernails by scraping at the lichen formations, I hear a nervy warning from behind: 'Daddy! Don't touch!' It was bad enough that we'd climbed the fence to enter Peter's private patch. Further delay to take photos heightened the sense of alarm. A couple of curious schoolmates wavered and watched, delaying the morning drop-off.

In 1833, Saint Peter's name was given to a Catholic school newly established in Aberdeen, where,

some 177 years later, my son began his primary education. And since then, Saint Peter has been an ordinary reference point in the rhythms of our family's conversation. His name is stitched into the school crest (just above the motto *Religioni et Bonis Moribus*) appearing on the items of uniform, laundered and in need of folding, near to where I write. But being the atheist half of our son's parentage, prior to beginning this short essay I had found no compelling reason to give the saint, his life or the school's nomination very much depth of thought. And nor had I made the most obvious geographical link, connecting two educational institutions, both operating under the auspices of the Roman Catholic Church, that gradually I am coming to know better. Two places of learning and opportunity, located across country: a faith school found furthest East, and a once-was theological college, now obscured from view, in the overgrown edgelands of Greater Glasgow. Truth to tell, the world is full of such St Peter's. The results of a quick web search suggest that, had I time or inclination, a global map of his influence could be

charted. Coloured pins might point up a nominal constellation: my son's school numbering alongside many hundred others, and that's before beginning on the built heritage of basilicas, cathedrals, churches, hospitals, seminaries and roads.

But over dinner, on the same day as our hurried survey of the statue – and still in a state of ignorant bliss – I asked if Peter had any defining features so that I might begin to know him a little better.
'He holds the keys to the kingdom!' came the incredulous reply.
'Aahaaah. The man at the Pearly Gates, right? *Now* I see! Of course he does, of course he does.'

## Time's Arrow

St Peter's Seminary is a place that seems to have existed forever on the threshold. In the world that bore this new college, the future was something tangible, a vision right there in front of your eyes. Architecturally it was composed in bold lines, so as to enable theological preparations that would

embolden young men's lives with a mission. You can see this visionary potential in the self-assured swish of movement and easy exchanges among the trainee priests, all captured in the patient tracking and quiet holds of Murray Grigor's celebrated camerawork. Noviciates they might have been, but all apparently steadfast in the belief that they were heading for the divine life, and a future that would look after itself quite comfortably, thank you.

But with premature mouldering brought on by a West Atlantic atmosphere, compounded by marginalising effects felt from changing Vatican priorities, the building met with its future much earlier than anyone had ever envisaged. Neither architects nor Archdiocese foresaw a finale that would arrive so soon. But this has proved to be the oddest of end games; long-winded and asymptotic, never quite finding the means properly to play itself out. Like so many other modernist icons in the British landscape, St Peter's has endured the grand drift-promise of a salvage-salvation job, and with it a just-possible return to former glories. For decades,

a succession of happily-ever-afters have tantalised without ever much in the way of firm foundation. And as each new dawn is endlessly deferred, the real finality of demolition has hung about, proving the most pervasive and perennial of possibilities. And all around, during the downtimes, in the dank places, scaling the heights, there is the slow creep of entropy. Interrupted, once in a while, by bursts of wilful destruction, suddenly accelerating the stretched-out seasons of benign neglect.

For a few alt-tribes, who choose to navigate by different castes of mind, St Peter's is another kind of portal altogether. The site sounds a siren call for the retrospective personality, seducing fellow travellers and modern antiquarians eager to head off in the *opposite* direction. Across the years, it has evolved its own human ecology: the art and architecture school students, the pilgrims, the lone wolves, the super-fans, the neo-landscape painters, the 'urb-ex' gang, the ritualists, the psycho-geographers, and a medley of lesser-spotted misfits and bampots. For them, time's arrow points backwards, to a place where versions of the past can be revisited. If the grounds of the Kilmahew estate are the land that the powers-that-be tried their damndest to forget, for outsider groups and niche interests these premises open out into a vast structure of recollection. Among the

ruins, personalised pathways materialise, leading to mythologised, non-existent pasts. In lairs and hidden quarters, the cine-camera craft and spray-can art is darkly shaded. Between the concrete uprights and alignments, there are glimpses of tormented inscapes, worrisome chinks into secret worlds. The sense of loss multiplies with every mark made, like spores, entering into the lurid tags and stencilled motifs. And yet, even if these powerful elegies and imaginaries already seem to crowd the building's derelict, defaced shell, and disquiet its green estate, *now* more than ever seems the moment for the configuration of something truly different.

## *What Next?*

It really ought to be the question on the tip of everyone's tongue. Ours is the on-the-cusp era. We've no shortage of reasons to be anxious and anticipatory, properly fearful of slipping over an ecological threshold that offers no hope of return. The Future, twenty-first-century style, is heavily contingent, already burdened. Best-case scenario – condition critical. Unlike earlier utopian models, today's tomorrow promises a less amenable environment, and a less predictable climate. The 'no point dwelling on it' brigade is keen that tales of end-times and eco-catastrophe get muffled, or

quickly transformed into corporate opportunities for all tomorrow's parties that are more bravely 'future-facing'. But that compromised version of green won't wash.

Better to find some incentive for progressive action around the pressing issues of our time; a bridging point between global predicament and home turf; a direct way to regain some local ground; a place for people to wrestle back the initiative; a home into which all that nervous energy might be invested, and aimed at producing creative and compelling kinds of environmental and community expression. Somewhere tangible, poignant and political: a place for doing. Somewhere culturally valued, and making valuable contribution. St Peter's might not yet be a landscape fit for purpose, but it's got all the makings to be put right back on the map. And, for a preciously short window of time, NVA has the keys to the kingdom.

All sorts of pragmatic 'what next?' will soon populate the blank expanse of such grand ambition. Quite right too; the sooner the better, in fact. There are a multitude of site-specific matters arising, each calling on a knowledge of local particulars, and an intimacy with the social geography to be found on the ground. What will be the pace of change?

Who will contribute? Who will document the process? What will become of the memories? And the material relics? How will things be made safe, but keep their edge? Who'll delineate the physical limits? And the symbolic ones? Who will visit? How will they arrive? And depart? In what combination? And at whose invitation? Or commission? What kinds of learning will be encouraged? For whose benefit? How will lives, young and old, be emboldened? According to what systems of value? There are no easy answers to such questions, and probably no consensus. The communities and publics soon to enter into the regeneration of St Peter's are diverse, and differently scaled. There can be no guarantee of a continuously happy valley. Fortunate then that tension is no stranger to the site.

It's time to imagine and re-invent, among the trees, living for the future, and still longing for the past. An eventful, social and affirmative place: for stories, for movement, for inhabiting, for advocacy, for re-discovery, for efficacy, for learning, for growing, for understanding, for experiment, for journeys and for encounters.

That's quite a lot to be *for*. And that's many St Peter's. It's a prospect to relish.

# Past and Future Use

We're not waiting for some perfect solution in the future, because even as it is, it has an enormous story to tell, otherwise we wouldn't be here. It's such a rich subject matter.

*Angus Farquhar*

Listening to the discussion and watching the film [*Space and Light* by Murray Grigor], the question that really struck me is: who is going to use it? How? In what way is it re-understood? And how is it going to relate to its immediate community?

*Adam Sutherland*

I don't think it's fair to refer to it just as a rich man's domain, because the original Kilmahew estate is part of our industrial heritage. It was founded by the son of the man who founded the Cunard Line, which was one of Glasgow's most successful shipping lines. Many of the shrubs and the trees in the forest are imported, and have survived, so they're a reminder of the lost industrial initiative that we once had in Scotland.

*Murray Grigor*

Because of the structure of spiritual places within the building, we keep coming back to monastic notions of a kind of sanctuary. That's not what it was. It was a place to basically train a highly skilled cadre that was then exported outwards. So, in a sense, if you're looking at it as a reflection of these pure origins, it was about the building of individuals with a range of skills; it was a model of the creation of complete people and the notion of the site as somewhere from which knowledge was exported. I think that is something we should keep reflecting on and remembering: it was a seminary, not a monastery.

*Moira Jeffrey*

We have to collectively nail our colours to the mast – and that requires a seriousness of intent and an intellectual clarity – so that a small nation that has not been used to making particularly radical decisions is capable and confident to take the step that is required to allow people like us to own places like St Peter's.

*Angus Farquhar*

If you really go back to the purpose of the site: it was for a seminary, it was a place of retreat, it was a place where a particular kind of education was delivered, where young men were taught to be priests in a very rarefied situation, in a landscape. They're all conscious decisions. It wasn't accidental that this building was built in the estate of a very rich person around a rather old Victorian house. So there is an important intellectual, political history about that site, and why it has achieved the stature it has. And anything that happens there, whatever it is, somehow has to tap into that, very carefully.

*Henry McKeown*

Design teams these days are not just architects and artists; they also consist of ecologists, writers, thinkers in all manner of ways. An interesting thing about the future of any project, never mind St Peter's, is the importance of landscape architects and ecologists, environmental scientists etc., who are all playing a part in that process.

*Alan Pert*

It was designed as a seminary for Catholic priests and the desirability or the possibility of restoring that function has gone. And once the function of a building has gone (and we are sitting in one in exactly that situation [a former church in Venice]), the form of that building I suppose has a curious effect on what happens next. It can't dictate what happens next, because to take the Corbusian analogy of the building growing around the function doesn't mean that you can do it the other way round: the function growing around the building. It is not the same sort of relationship, but it sort of leads or steers things in a curious direction. One of the really interesting things is that it is a project that has no brief and nobody knows what it is going to be like. That allows the building to sort of change incrementally, as it has been ruined incrementally.

*Edward Hollis*

The idea that you could latch onto the idea of learning and the idea of it being so important to the teaching of young people is for me critical; that makes it very engaging. But the question is: what is the end game? If you are going to chase that dream, you have to have a more concrete notion of what the outcomes might be.

*Henry McKeown*

We need an interpretation, which can be not a technical one, but it must be a political interpretation, or a cultural interpretation. But the more important thing is that it must be adopted by more than one decision. To be able to take the right decision and not the wrong decision, and to have time to do that, you have to use these kinds of instruments to create a meeting point.

*Leonardo Ciacci*

When it was first declared surplus to requirements, it wasn't really thought of as a massive issue. The idea was, 'We'll sell this building', and there was interest from hoteliers. Then there was a scheme to turn it into five townhouses. If that had happened, then we would have lost it. So the idea of there being a solution at the time could have been quite destructive, and there were other similar schemes which didn't go ahead. We should be glad now that they didn't go ahead.

*Ranald MacInnes*

Thirty years ago nobody was interested in Mackintosh, and now that situation is completely different. So things change, and the context and the way in which we think about preservation changes as well. What Rem Koolhaas is talking about [in his exhibit at the Biennale] is that there is always an economic envelope that will actually guide the thinking about what will happen, in terms of preservation. Three or four years ago, for example, it might have been possible to think about some other kind of (commercial) intervention at St Peter's, which was about seeing the potential of the site with regards to making something out of it, and that would have taken you down a completely different route. That economic envelope doesn't exist anymore, and this may be a good thing.

*Ian Gilzean*

We've been talking about remembering the function, and, of course, the building only exists in the form that it does because of the function. This is an understanding that is all wrapped up in the statement of significance, which is part of the 2008 Avanti report. A statement like that is supposed to inform what you do with the building thereafter, so if some major intervention is needed, that intervention is then to be justified in relation to the relative significance of the architecture. So the nature of possibilities is very much related to the function of the building and can't really be forgotten.

*Ranald MacInnes*

St Peter's is not a place where I might feel comfortable or welcomed in its original function. We have been talking quite a lot about function. But if you see the figures moving through space [in Murray Grigor's film], within the limits of ritualised space, the male figures have a certain amount of room. The women are all in darkness and domestic spaces. I have been trying to think through what it means that many of these physical spaces now have simply been blown open, or blown apart by the process of ruination. There were a couple of shots where I suddenly thought there is an amazing potential in the opening out of the building, in that simple physical way.

*Moira Jeffrey*

I am really fascinated by the whole idea that this is about process and that there isn't an end use. The process is the thing that is driving it. Remembering the conversation about how the Church think nothing of a hundred years. Thinking of an end use: it might not happen in our lifetime; and that is fine.

*Morag Bain*

We've been in a situation in which there has been a passive kind of neglect and we have moved to one in which we are going to have active engagement. It may be modest, it may be incremental, but it starts us on a journey, I think that is the point. We are at the start of a new journey.

*Ian Gilzean*

I think taking what exists and enhancing it is a good idea. It was a school. It has the estate and context, which is an interesting one. It should really be a school again. A lot of what is being put forward as potential use is a kind of super school. The language around schools is almost impossible to use, because it has been so twisted. A school of a much broader realm of education, a reinvention of what we mean by schools, seems a good way to do it. The rest is detail.

*Adam Sutherland*

When one is talking about open-ended process and consultation and collaboration, you still get to the point where somebody has got to make a decision and say, 'This needs to happen'. Communities aren't just happy groupings of people who all agree with each other. If one is going to follow what people are doing, to start this open-ended process, but what has happened so far has been vandalism, then how do you steer it? At what point does a process itself need to be designed?

*Edward Hollis*

St Peter's has a strong potential to educate people, who are not tourists, who do not have a specific use for the place. But they can be open to many different levels of relationship with that place. Education is a way to give people instruments to be active in their own reality.

*Leonardo Ciacci*

The proposition about the future function and activity of the building will arise from the landscape, and that is really the driver of change in activity.

*Rolf Roscher*

Individual locomotion is a way to think creatively once again about how the site might be re-inhabited. We could quite usefully revisit older walking traditions that Scotland has as a nation: customary rights of beating bounds, the idea of retaining public access, not just in linear terms but actually in broad aerial terms. There are lots of ways in which Scotland can remember something more of its pedestrian past, and all of those kinds of walking practices are very timely. It speaks to agendas of health and wellbeing, but it is also a way for people to ventilate ideas and ventilate their own experience.

*Hayden Lorimer*

This will be a walked landscape and the building will be part of a walked landscape. The act of walking is non-passive. Observing the world through the act of moving through it becomes an end in itself, and through allowing that to become serious again, it's a chance to step outside societal norms. Perhaps this is a utopian principle, but I don't think this is a romantic gesture. This is about basic human need.

*Angus Farquhar*

A community is not one thing and one opinion, it's an endless diversity, and there are tensions and arguments within the communities and disagreements. That's democratic life. So rather than attempting to homogenise and make everyone into a perfect community that uses it in a safe and perfect way, you're releasing the potential for people to feel comfortable or uncomfortable within this. For us, it's very important then to respect this plurality of visions.

*Angus Farquhar*

NVA have said they want to give people the space to make their own narrative, and I think that can lead to what a school, whatever you mean by school, could be. It is about exploring yourself and finding out stuff, so it is about making your own story. It is a place for imagination and challenges for yourself.

*Morag Bain*

You cannot divorce from the purpose of that architecture, whether it is institutional or not, or whether it is collective or not, because the collective memory of that site is bound up in that building. Therefore anything that happens has to be bound into that in some way.

*Henry McKeown*

It's not a process of us becoming tied into a sort of exploitation of individuals who must pay vast sums of money in order for us to impart wisdom. It should be the inverse of this approach. It is to create places where the subject matter is so interesting and so rich that you would simply use great minds from many different disciplines to allow people to draw what they can from this narrative. Maybe it is about teaching people to grow vegetables; that is as important as understanding the tradition of Ruskin and Scarpa and Le Corbusier and Mackintosh and how their lineage runs through the building.

*Angus Farquhar*

## On the Ruin's Future: Keeping Things Open

### Emma Cocker

A proposition: Located at and provoked by the site of the Grade A listed St Peter's Seminary, a modernist ruin in the heart of the Kilmahew Estate, *On the Ruin's Future: Keeping Things Open* is conceived as a discursive *event*, bringing together different positions and perspectives to question and interrogate the potentiality – as well as the problematic – of the architectural ruin. This event explores the possibility of different *openings* (and notions of *openness*), to initiate and invite debate around the ruin and the proposed redevelopment of the St Peter's site. Presentations will be situated in different geographical locations within St Peter's (see map for location details); a peripatetic audience will engage with ideas simultaneously to a live encounter with the site. The event will begin as dawn breaks and continue as long as the light lasts and weather permits. Audience may come and go as they wish.

.................................................................................
.................................................................................

### ① The Ruins Look Back[i]

*'These ruins are situated on the bank of a winding river. The climate is nondescript. To the South-West there rises a metallic construction with openings, very high, and whose purpose we haven't been able to determine'.*

Reflecting on Robert Desnos' surrealist poem, *Mourning for Mourning* [Deuil pour Deuil] (1924), Mary Ann Caws explores the figure of the ruin within surrealism, tracing its presence through texts such as Benjamin Péret's 'On the Ruin of Ruins' in *Minotaure* back towards potential surrealist precursors

such as François de Nomé's *A City in Ruins at Night* (1625–30). She states, 'Like some gigantic De Chirico painting, these ruins, metaphoric and metaphysical, are inscribed with a deep anxiety, pervaded by a sinister unknown. The celebration of this site at once abandoned and undone calls forth a poetry rife with a panic both past and future […] what is presented as a not-knowing and an undoing, the enigmatic remains of the past successfully defeat any possibility of present or future knowledge […] The anxious desire to know how something is used (*l'usage*) is situated as far as possible from the surrealist celebration of open and unspecified expectation (*l' état d'attente*), that expecting just of always expecting.'[ii] The intent is to elaborate on Caws' idea of the ruin as a site of 'unspecified expectation' (*l' état d'attente*), whose indeterminacy operates as a block or obstacle to those forms of knowing and naming predicated on establishing stable terms of use or function. Exploring both the potential and the problematic of the ruin's *openness*, the ruin will be examined on the basis of its refusal to fully perform according to the laws of either utility or ornament. The ruin calls for other ways of thinking and knowing, placing emphasis on processes and practices of 'not-knowing' and of 'undoing' rather than of fixing and defining. Rather than trying to reassemble or recollect the ruin back into some illusory whole (returning a sense of its former use and structure, now long since past or collapsed), questioning turns to explore what it means to dwell in the uncertainty or indeterminacy of architectural ruins or remnants, or rather what does it mean to leave something *open*? Here, the term *nondescript* is recuperated from its pejorative meaning (as in 'lacking distinctive or interesting features or characteristics') and explored for its capacity to reflect the ruin's status as 'not easily classified', its refusal or resistance to singular or stable forms of description.

.................................................................................
.................................................................................

## ② *Being Left Open – Ruin as an Open Structure*

Proposing the notion of the ruin as an open structure, the tension between openness as an expansive *modus operandi* that supports multi-use or purpose and the attendant risks and responsibilities therein will be explored. Being open can signal towards a neutral state or the capacity for polyvalence, for manifold meaning. It is *(a)* not shut or closed; *(b)* having no protecting or concealing cover; *(c)* carried on in full view; *(d)* not closely defended by an opponent; *(e)* not sealed or tied; *(f)* having interspersed gaps, spaces, or intervals; *(g)* accessible; *(h)* free from limitations, boundaries or restrictions; *(i)* to speak freely and candidly; *(j)* to open (one's) eyes, to become aware of the truth of a situation; *(k)* willing to consider or deal with something; *(l)* ready to transact business; *(m)* not yet decided, subject to further thought; *(n)* characterised by lack of pretense or reserve, frank; *(o)* free of prejudice, receptive to new ideas and understanding; *(p)* generous; *(q)* in operation, live; *(r)* to *undo*, to release from a closed or fastened position; *(s)* to remove obstructions from, clear; *(t)* to get (something) going, initiate; *(u)* to make or force an opening or gap in, to break the continuity of; *(v)* to make more responsive or understanding; *(w)* to reveal the secrets of, to bare; *(x)* to modify (one's stance); *(y)* to accelerate; *(z)* susceptible, vulnerable. Open space is that which has yet to be territorialised, brought under private own. However, with openness comes vulnerability, for a space can soon become unruly in the absence of any rule. To leave something open thus carries an attendant risk, for it is an unprotected state whose facing edges remain exposed. The ruin is a site most marginal; its identity shaped by the exposure of its open(ed) interiors and its perception of the risk therein. Danger might be averted by protecting this raw edge, or by treating it as an open wound or sore. However, the covered wound is often prone to fester; better then to trust it to the good of the air. Resistance is the tolerance garnered through an encounter with minor risk and danger; not the fear fostered in the attempt to maintain one's distance, keep peril at bay. The intent is to advocate a model of openness based on resilience with receptivity. To be open affirms the value of what cannot be planned or prepared for, rather than closing things down in an attempt to legislate or defend against.

........................................................................................
........................................................................................

## ③ *Ruin – The Suspended Potentiality of Narrative Stalled*

Ruin describes both the event itself (ruin as verb) and its subsequent residue (ruin as noun). It is a persisting remainder or reminder of a trajectory of action suspended or ceased part way through, a break or rupture in the teleological timeline of events, progress stalled. Reflecting on the work of contemporary artists such as Tacita Dean, the figure of the ruin is interrogated for its capacity to extend or develop the vocabulary for reflecting on the potentiality of failure, irresolution and open-endedness. Clarrie Wallis states, 'The *relic*, as dislocated from an original signifying context which is now lost, is central to Dean's work: we are shown objects and places that are charged with meaning that we cannot fully read, often depicting a failed or abandoned vision.'[iii] The deserted and half-complete remnant of *Bubble House* (1999) is captured on film by Dean, encountered accidently by the artist on the Cayman Brac while making her filmic portrait of the shipwreck, or *marine* ruin, *Teignmouth Electron*. *Sound Mirrors* (1999) further reflects her interest in depicting a failed or abandoned vision; the film presents images and sounds gleaned from the site of a number of World War I listening devices at Denge near Dungeness, whose incapacity to discriminate *between* sounds resulted in them soon falling out of use. Dean's practice is one of resuscitation and rescue, where forgotten or unfulfilled narratives from the past serve as the impetus for a quest in which she can be seen as a detective or archivist piecing together fragments of history. However, rather than trying to re-produce a coherent narrative or historical account of events, Dean approaches the ruin as a partial fragment of a broken or unfulfilled narrative, a loose end into which she weaves other, tangential *asides*. She does not wish to retell the past, but rather her investigation exists in the 'present tense … it is about now and all that *still* resonates.' Hers is a makeshift or bricolaged narrative, emerging at the interstice between fictional, autobiographical and documentary perspectives. Dean's work attests to the potentiality of the ruin as an 'unfulfilled beginning', whose past refuses to be pieced back together as a coherent history or whole, but is instead used as a starting point for developing new narratives, new stories about place. For Michel de Certeau, 'stories about places' are always provisional and incomplete; they are of an 'order' that is 'everywhere punched and torn open by ellipses, drifts, and leaks of meaning: it is a sieve-order.'[iv]

⊗ *Performing Ruin*

*Various sites, unscheduled*: Following Anne Eggebert and Sarah Cole's work, *Folly* (2009), the ruin is taken as an obstacle course or improvised gymnasium against which a team of *traceurs* practise a live display of *parkour*. St Peter's is investigated as a site of critical leverage or pressure against which to work, where obstacles within the landscape operate as productive constraints that necessitate unexpected ways of being or behaving. This performance is set against the conceptual backdrop of *The Architectural Body* (2002) by architectural theorists Arakawa + Gins, an elaboration on how the navigation of obstacles involves a critical engagement with one's environment, forcing the emergence of new tactical ways of operating.

④ *No Longer and Not Yet*

The status of the ruin is one of exemption; it is a liminal structure, 'no longer classified and not yet classified'.[v] While the term 'liminality' originally referred to the transitional phase of a rite of passage or ritual, its meaning has been expanded to include states, places, people or conditions determined by their structural ambiguity or quality of inbetweenness, their position on the 'threshold' of or between two different existential planes. Liminality is often applied to situations where the laws and logic that habitually govern reality falter or fail to apply. Victor Turner describes how during the liminal phase of ritual performance the characteristics of the social structure are no longer and not yet applicable as ritual subjects 'pass through a period and area of ambiguity'.[vi] During this phase, it becomes possible for the 'liminal person' to momentarily escape the rules and regulations of a given society, the terms of the ritual providing a kind of exemption from habitual logic. Here, the initiate or novice remains 'temporarily undefined, beyond the normative social structure'.[vii] Perhaps then, it is possible to conceive of the ruin in analogous terms to the initiate within Turner's ritual. The ruin is suspended between times. It is no longer required to perform the utilitarian function for which it was originally designed, but has not yet been designated a new role or purpose. Here, this seeming *redundancy* produces a creative hiatus or pause, a space in which to conceive things as otherwise before a new use or function has been fully determined. The intent then is to reflect on the critical potentiality made possible within the liminal phase of ritual, exploring whether these affordances might be extended (more permanently) to the site of the ruin. Focus is placed on exploring the critical value of 'un-belonging' within liminality, of momentarily operating beyond the laws and logic that govern reality (both past and the future), in order to gain access to what Turner would call 'anti-structure', the 'subjunctive world' of the liminal phase. The 'subjunctive' mood of a verb is used to express supposition, desire, hypothesis, or possibility. Turner notes that the subjunctive 'is a world of "as if" … It is "if it *were* so", not "it *is* so".'[viii] The subjunctive nature of liminality invites towards a process of thinking differently and of seeing things differently. Extending the logic of the subjunctive to the site of the ruin is thus to frame such spaces as active places of questioning and imagining, of performing 'as if' rather than 'it is'.

........................................................................

## ⑤ *Becoming Cuckoo: How to Preoccupy Site*

Landscapes loop to the eternal rhythm of rise and decline, endlessly enacting the cycle of dereliction and regeneration, of ruin and rebirth. Every burgeoning venture has already begun to run its course, while obsolescence is the germinal ground upon which new emergence roots. Between one round of development and the next, there is often a brief interval wherein a space or situation exists between contracts, where space becomes momentarily deterritorialised, unbound. Temporal margins open up a window of opportunity. Timely interventions can be made to stall progress, enabling the site to pause and catch its breath. Reflecting on various

artists' interventions into sites of proposed regeneration or redevelopment, the aim is to explore how the notion of 'preoccupation' can function as a mode of critical site-specificity. While preoccupation describes a state of mental absorption, it can also mean the physical act of occupying or taking possession of something before someone else. The cuckoo harnesses the potential of this double meaning, attempting to preoccupy both its host's attention and the physical space within its nest […] Akin to the dissenting squatter, an artist's attempt to preoccupy a site is a resistant tactic for preventing it from other uses. Preoccupation points to an illicit species of occupation that insinuates itself before more legitimate or productive forms have taken hold. Its occupation is of an improper, dysfunctional, all-consuming kind; it distracts the event of other, more useful or permissible kinds of activity. Preoccupation takes possession in advance of official or designated use; it is the tender trespass of a site that wishes for it to remain open. To inhabit a ruin in a way that precludes other usage emerges as a way of preventing it from the insensitive regeneration that so many other such buildings have been subjected to. Inhabiting a ruin (without regenerating it or returning too much of a use) can be understood as an attempt to extend or maintain this state of pause or suspension (if only temporarily), transforming its disused structure into a space of latent possibility or potentiality.

........................................................................

## ⑥ *Twelve Categories: Classifying the Unclassified and Unclassifiable*

The ruin is tested against Francesco Orlando's 'Twelve Categories' of decay and obsolescence as outlined in his publication, *Obsolete Objects in the Literary Imagination: Ruins, Relics, Rarities,*

*Rubbish, Uninhabited Places, and Hidden Treasures.*
The categories, which Orlando asserts are 'not
to be too sharply distinguished', include the
solemn-admonitory, the threadbare-grotesque,
the venerable-regressive, the worn-realistic,
the reminiscent-affective, the desolate-
disconnected, the magico-superstitious, the
sinister-terrifying, the precious-potential, the
sterile-noxious, the prestigious-ornamental
and the pretentious-fictitious. In attempting to
classify the seemingly unclassifiable properties
of the ruin within this extended taxonomy of
the decayed and discarded, the intent is to
develop a more nuanced understanding of
why and how the ruin has remained a charged
motif within contemporary times. Moreover, the
aim is to investigate why certain uninhabitable
architectures are deemed ruined while other
become ruins; why some are considered eyesores
while others are attributed the status of tourist
sites; why some ruins can stay ruins while others
are subjected to regeneration or swiftly knocked
down.

## ⑦ *<Inside>Outside<Inside>*

Taking the form of a cinematic essay, images
of various ruins are gathered to reflect upon
the spatial ambiguity of such sites, where the
habitual binary relation between notions of
inside and outside becomes wilfully collapsed.
The spatial organisation of the ruin is proposed
as a form of Möbius strip where inside and
outside no longer function as separate states
but rather bleed into and share the properties
of one another. Interior and exterior spaces
cannot be distinguished, but are perceived
simultaneously, encountered in the process of
becoming one.

## ⑧ *Beautiful Brutal: The Curious Lure of 'Béton Brut'*

With reference to selected artists' practice, the
specificity of the modernist – or even Brutalist
– ruin is examined as a site of contradiction,
oscillating between the utopian ambitions of its
conception and its failure to survive or withstand
human inhabitation. It is simultaneously potent
*and* impotent, simultaneously charged and
depleted of power. Connections are drawn
between Sean Edwards' recent treatment of
the Maelfa shopping centre near Cardiff; Karin
Kihlberg and Reuben Henry's interest in and
investigation of Birmingham Central Library
through their multi-screen video work *Inbindable
Volume,* and the artists' publication, *Misleading
Epiphenomena,* by Dutton + Swindells in dialogue
with architect Barbara Penner, which takes
Park Hill Flats, Sheffield, as the 'prompt for
observations and conversations, addressing
questions of northern identity, architectural
modernism, corporation, social housing and
entropy'. Product of the utopian optimism
of the post-war period, Maelfa, Birmingham
Central Library and Park Hill Flats (like many
other architectural projects of this period) never
fulfilled their planners' hopes, each falling
foul of decline (or of public dissatisfaction or
derision) even while in development. Yet the
modernist ruin continues to display complex
enigmatic (or even *aporetic*) properties, creating
a conceptual impasse through the co-existence
of endeavour and resignation, of hope and
failure, of presence and absence therein. It
is perhaps these unstable or even *multi-stable*
possibilities that make the ruin (or the process
of a building 'becoming a ruin', to follow Robert
Smithson) an ongoing point of provocation for
artists.

## ⑨ The 'She' of Ruin

Addressing the more problematic aspects of the ruin (and the broader phenomenon of *atephilia*), comparisons are made between the romanticisation of the architectural ruin and that of other ruined figures. Drawing on Elizabeth Bronfen's *Over Her Dead Body: Death, Femininity and the Aesthetic*, the intent is to demonstrate connections and parallels between interest in the figure of the ruin and the ruined woman within Romanticism and beyond. For Bronfen, the trope of female death, dereliction or abandonment operates as a site of 'otherness' against which a counter position of masculine strength and vitality (images of male health, energy, exuberance, power, virility) is reinforced. Arguably, the ruin functions in analogous terms, where it is often considered in need of rescue or redemption, or else approached through the exertion or exercise of a certain kind of bravado played out through a flirtation with its more dangerous or dubious elements. Bronfen's text becomes used as a point of provocation from which to begin to tease out and untangle intriguing (if rather under-explored) gendered arguments that lurk beneath the surface of contemporary debates around the ruin.

## ⑩ Open Poetics

To refer to the poetics of the ruin is not to describe it adjectivally, even pejoratively, but instead signals towards the critical nature of its open-endedness, the unresolved or unfixed relationship between its fragmentary parts. The term 'poetics' is not used to evoke the sensibility or quality of the ruin within poetic representation, but rather intimates towards the making and unmaking of the ruin; its construction through processes of de-construction and re-construction. Architectural theorist Jan Turnovský has noted how, 'Poetics is related etymologically to the Greek term *poiein*, which means "to make". This is the root of the term *poiesis*: fabrication, production.' He adds that, 'The maxim of the poetic is not to fix meaning but to offer a choice of possibilities – an indeterminate open-endedness.'[ix] Bringing Turnovský's poetic 'open-endedness' into dialogue with other theoretical writing, including Umberto Eco's *The Open Work* (1989), and poet Charles Olson's proposal of *Projective Verse* (1950) (which conceives of text as OPEN by emphasising the relation of breath to writing), the intent is to elaborate the notion of the ruin as a form of 'open text', whose meaning perpetually shimmers between the determinacy of its former function and the unspecified or indeterminate potential of its current form.

*Endnotes*

i Mary Ann Caws, *The Surrealist Look: An Erotics of Encounter* (Cambridge, MA: MIT Press, 1997) p. 303.

ii Ibid, pp. 153–5.

iii Clarrie Wallis, 'Introduction', *Tacita Dean* (London: Tate Publishing, 2001) p. 9.

iv Michel de Certeau, *The Practice of Everyday Life*, trans. Steven Rendall (Berkeley, CA: University of California Press, 1984) p. 107.

v Victor Turner, *The Forest of Symbols: Aspects of Ndembu Ritual* (Ithaca: Cornell University Press, 1967) p. 96.

vi Ibid, p. 24.

vii Ibid, p. 27.

viii Ibid, pp. 82–3.

ix Jan Turnovský, *The Poetics of a Wall Projection* (London: Architectural Association, 2009 / 1987) p. 83.

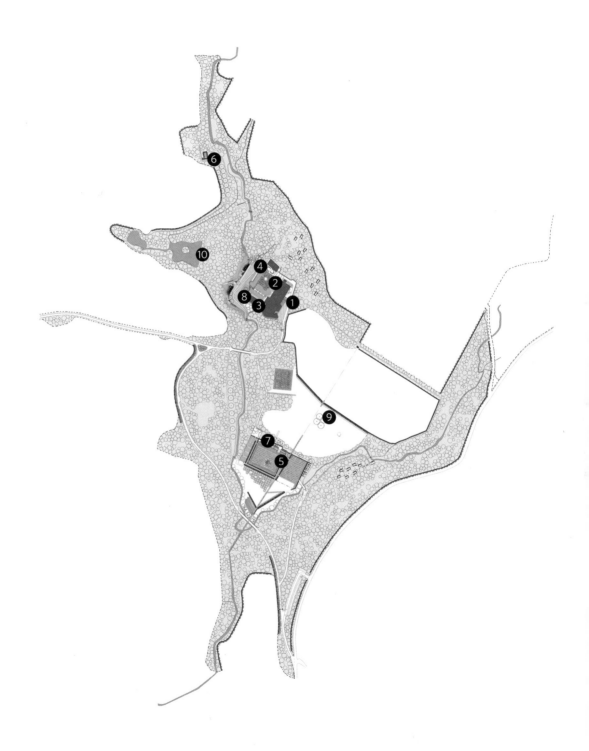

# Function and Use

The thing that attracts people to a site is its controversy. This site is unique and controversial.

I fear that it'll take off in a large way [and ruin the site].

Kilmahew is a place for peace and to empty my head – keep the private areas.

Local history is rarely ever studied in schools, and it is such a great thing for children. There is so much of it here that they don't know about.

The site certainly has an almost spiritual aspect. Even before it was owned by the Catholic Church it was used as a holy site. It would be nice to try and keep that sense of the 'spiritual'.

There is scope for some sculptural elements to be introduced in the landscape – either temporary or permanent.

There are a number of areas that could be used for outdoor performances.

I see the young enjoying the adventure. I hope that this discovery and adventure aspect will not be lost in any plans.

We don't want a country / theme park.

Not knowing much about the trails available to take or the general history of the site, it would be good to be able to gather a bit of knowledge along the way.

Local re-organisation has meant that the local archives have been scattered so our history has become fragmented. Now we could bring it back together and make it complete again.

There is the appetite to set something up through heritage for the village as a whole, to gather information, for something that is community based.

It's not just about documenting the past, we should be capturing it as it is now, as nature has taken it over.

# A Conversation

**Ed Hollis**: Maybe we can start by summarising where things are now. What has happened since the debate in Venice?

**Angus Farquhar**: We've bought the site and the buildings; our offer was accepted and we have a two-year period in which to further develop our plans. We are halfway through the articulation of a masterplan with Avanti and ERZ, and our approach is to develop a number of phases. Depending on what funding is raised we can decide what to do when. In terms of usage, we are looking at the minimum we require as a shelter, for basic facilities and power, to allow a successful start to a programme, so we don't have to wait for phase two. There is a set of operational decisions to be made; we know that for the site to be safe people have to stay there, so that defines the need for sleeping accommodation. To reverse nearly thirty years of abandonment you have to people that landscape, with a gradual process of realisation that it has become worth keeping.

**EH**: It is quite a big first move, to have people sleeping there, inhabiting the site.

**AF**: We want to have a base there, a place to bring people, where we can hold meetings, host crew, deal with site management, so that defines the function of some of the building. The most important decision as a matter of choice is that we want to counterbalance the consolidated form by a partially or fully restored form in the buildings. That juxtaposition is quite harsh, so what is clearly temporary ('unsightly aid') is treated as something that can be designed to be actively seen for the first few years of its life.

Particularly in the main block, the mix of quite a raw treatment of the refectory space against a restored chapel is the route that we are going down, so that we have a fully functioning flexible wind- and watertight space that is surprisingly beautiful in terms of its interior compared to its exterior. The refectory should remain open to the elements. We

neither re-glaze nor seal; we leave it open and keep the trees naturally coming up to it.

**EH**: So it becomes a building that starts out fully dressed and ends up naked and fades away.

**AF**: It's to acknowledge the value of the process of ruination and to allow that quality to permeate it, so you are always aware of the restored element within something that is already partially lost. We are not setting out to make a perfect vision of the future in architectural terms, or in the way we set to critique the notion of a learning centre. It's been one of the criticisms of early stages of modernism; so we accept failure as a valid comment.

**EH**: I'm interested in addressing the idea of restoring one part and conserving the other. This taps into a whole nineteenth-century idea that the two don't meet. It is an interesting idea to put both together in this broken machine. I find the most provocative bit the restoration. Are you restoring it as a chapel?

**AF**: The chapel is deconsecrated, but there is no doubt that the main internal spaces carry residues of their prior use. That's definitely a question to be addressed; for example, where there was an organ loft, we could put performance systems in. That represents a pragmatic use of space to fulfil the function we now require. There is a question about the sanctuary space, which is often seen as shrouded, or screened from outside. You can't see out, apart from upwards through the roof space above the altar, through which light was modified by a strange ziggurat rooflight. To make a completely secluded space is less relevant to us, as we won't be performing Mass, so maybe it will be interesting to have greater permeability and get a sense of self in the context of a wider skeletal structure. That raises architectural questions about whether we are willing to violate the purity of a restored form, and we are!

**EH**: That is always the issue of restoration; it implies there was an original of something designed in one go. The idea of partial restoration allows the question to be ventilated.

AF: Our aim is to make a workable space with a remarkable atmosphere and history; for it to also have a remarkable future it needs to be usable. From the beginning I felt it should not be something set in one period. It should be a space where, if appropriate, a contemporary architectural intervention can happen, so the interior space finds its own balance and sense of complexity.

EH: A schoolboy question is: what happens to the altar in a place like this?

AF: One of the strongest images that implies desecration is the broken altar. It feels like it is the result of an intentional act. In knitting that altar back together, we feel it is just as important to show the stitches, not to smooth it over, but to show what it has gone through. And it should stay: to take it out would create a strange emptiness.

While there isn't an overt spiritual agenda, we could position the chapel as a secular or multi-faith resource, where the solemnity and quality of silence within it could be used to help remember someone's life, for instance; there are echoes of function that we will pick up and build on without mimicry.

EH: That brings us back to the idea that the building started like a machine that had specific parts doing specific things. As a ruin it has ceased to be that, but a ruin's meaning or reading isn't completely open-ended; it tells you things about what it used to be. It's a question of getting the building to tell you what it wants to be, but not instantly restoring it back to machine ...

AF: The problem with St Peter's is that it was not necessarily loved. There is no doubt that there were days and Masses in the sanctuary that are still indelibly imprinted in people's memories after thirty or forty years. That is one thing I want to find out: at a point in history, when some of the social hierarchies were beginning to break down after World War II, how could a building this ambitious and optimistic about the future be built? When we say we don't live in times like that, weren't they just as insecure? Isn't that just an illusion we project onto modernism, that it somehow had a sense of the future we don't feel anymore?

EH: It is amazing when you think of the pessimistic optimism of rebuilding the world that was bombed and devastated. St Peter's was borne out of the same notion of necessity; not as a self-indulgent private artwork. Training priests to go into the community is based on the notion of it being a model community itself. One of the strange things is that [at that time] people thought on a much larger scale.

AF: The buildings with vast interior scales now tend to be museums or arts centres, like Tate Modern, which reuse industrial cathedrals, which is a clear sign of a changing of the religious or work focus to cultural functions, and we are continuing in that vein. I don't sense a great deal of optimism about the future now. In the past decades there have been massive pockets of wealth creation, but that is not now feeding out into the wider society. That is why I liked the presentation on Lina Bo Bardi's work in Venice, and her idea of humble architecture, which seems appropriate to our time. Part of an incremental development through not having money to throw at a problem and make a hasty solution. If you have a fast solution you may rue the fact that you didn't take more time.

EH: Yes, you end up creating yourself a white elephant. Does the whole project feel different now that it's real? Do you find in a sense that the open-ended and iterative approach, allowing the project to grow, bit by bit, suddenly feels like a very different idea?

AF: We are now in a very practical phase and ideas have to stand up against these practicalities. Many publicly-funded solutions want outcomes with such sparkling clarity that some of the more open-ended approaches can seem vague rather than the best way to the right answer. It simply means you have to engage in this long, careful, pragmatic process, as you're talking about public money. Issues must be raised and answered effectively; there is a need to somehow 'project' a finished article.

EH: It is the process that makes it special. The way you describe the Commission Plan is like a process rather than a product.

AF: Yes, how you ask people to think about it along the way is important. When the masterplan is completed we will invite other people into a kind of peer review. It will take a temperature reading and ensure a conversation continues all the way through.

EH: It is interesting that you talk of peer review, rather than consultation. For a project like this, its critical reception is part of its job.

AF: Absolutely. The idea of it being alive now and out there, it already represents something that has a value, two years before a development does or doesn't take place. It's very important to keep that moving and to feed that. Rather than just treat it as a formal planning period and say, 'Consultation: done that'.

EF: This notion of criticism and critical reception is interesting. Walking on my way here I saw a poster that invites people to visit Glasgow and see its fine buildings. Twelve buildings were represented as paperweights drawn as objects, completely uncritically. They were a) not buildings in action, just paperweights and objects, and b) there was no criticism of their worth. It was more a checklist of Foster, Hadid etc., a collection; weird, as it has no relationship to how we use buildings in real life.

AF: When St Peter's was designed it was as a walk-through sculpture, as a series of activated dramatic spaces linked directly to how the seminarians would move through the rooms leading to Mass, the ritual centre of the seminary. That feels important to what we do and how we follow in that tradition; the idea of peripatetic learning is inherently, in newer language, all about embodiment and immersion ... Paul Stallan has said that architecture is an experience of form and our approach is about using architecture as a form of experience. It is about the act of thinking in spaces and how different spaces modulate your thinking, pull you in, or alienate

and set up perceptual questions that are not easily answered.

EH: John Summerson has written a lovely essay about ruins, stating that what is so lovely about them is that there are two types of ruins: one is not worth having, like the villa in Fishbourne in Sussex, with stones in lime but nothing else there. The other is where difficult judgement calls have to be made, and where there is just enough to think and reconstruct in your imagination. It is an interesting thought that there will still be spaces that one has to mentally complete, and others that are complete. Even in describing the chapel, there is a double experience of not form, but a double form of experience. You have several ways of reading something at the same time.

AF: The strangest fact is that the baronial house around which the modernist form wrapped has now gone, so you have this strange void. The landscape is full of absence; full of voided memory. So how you play with the traces can either reach a point where its disappearance leaves a sense of banality, or, at best, leaves you with a spark to think back through time. I was thinking of this notion of 'contested space'. If you go back to the fifteenth or sixteenth century, there was perhaps some form of manorial house and there was the classic Scottish castle or keep, with a very old 'right of way' down the side of the burn that would have linked Cardross village with markets along Loch Lomond and further North. So you can imagine that was very public, even though the keep would have had a private function. In the Victorian designed landscape, you have more of a sense of enclosure.

EH: It is almost a form of privatisation, isn't it?

AF: And yet, because the mid nineteenth-century owners, the Burns – who made their money through Cunard – were of that liberal, philanthropic tradition, it was relatively permeable. I don't know if it was generally 'open', but there were definitely paths laid out and there was public access, at times. So it wasn't the equivalent of a completely gated estate.

Then there was a whole period in which there was the semi-legal activity of poaching and fruit and vegetable raids by those with less money in the area – so there was that other form of permeability that has continued, through to the current feral state of the site as a ruin. Recently people have made it their own, and used it primarily as a cultural resource and an inspiration for their own work.

**EH**: What you are saying is that the site is not an enclosure, but it is a focus with varying degrees of permeability around it.

**AF**: It's never simply clear-cut. We have reached a point now at which we are attempting to give value and ownership to each visitor, who, as an active protagonist, takes the narrative on and decodes it on their own terms.

**EH**: Are you imagining or projecting that everybody who uses it actually steers its future in some way?

**AF**: I think that you have an absolute right to go there on a sunny day, walk your dog and have a cup of tea, and do whatever you want; but there will be a series of programmes that specifically invite your response. We might for example do a 'weekly run'.

**EH**: It's the new Mass!

**AF**: When you move and use other levels of physicality as you travel through that landscape, and invite others to do the same, you can build up a kind of physical cartography of the site. If you were to then simply document how it makes runners feel, what it makes them see and how they look at the phenomena around them and then recorded these reactions, you would already build an interesting resource. The idea is that there are a number of ways that ask for a more direct involvement.

**EH**: Any of the paths that people either make or that exist through that bit of land are very layered; some of them might be an old drovers' road, some of them might be an ornamental Victorian path, some of them might be something that somebody hacked through the undergrowth to go and smoke their weed – and each of those means something

very different as a path, as a route. Both in the sense of how it was established, and also in the sense that somebody who is walking down there now may have a completely different conception of what these paths mean. Perhaps the main thing to remember about paths is that they only exist because people use them; when they don't use them anymore then they disappear. You can see that in the Highlands every year; certain paths are just beaten down and over-walked, and some others simply peter out.

**AF**: ERZ's approach is that at times you don't just have to follow the straight line from A to B, and that routes can sometimes lead you into confusion, just fade away rather than lead to a set point, and to work *with* that as part of breaking the mould and being more playful with what you have within the landscape.

**EH**: But, who is it for? That is the question, isn't it?

**AF**: There are many ways in which people can learn, and there are many types of people we can learn from. I would like to see a flat structure where

someone who worked in the walled garden forty or fifty years ago, who has a particular perspective or light to throw on it will sit alongside an academic whose research is a response to modernism, entropy and ruination. They will be talking about the same period, but from radically opposite perspectives.

The implication therefore is that there isn't one way of doing something, there isn't one source – we keep coming back to that idea of multiplicity, or a pluralistic approach, and that it is important to explore this complexity.

Communities are often torn by arguments and division and have other moments when they coalesce in a really good way. What the story of St Peter's has done is bring some of those perspectives to the surface so it is very obvious that some love this building, some hate it, but there is a depth of feeling that is good to work with. It is not our role to paper over it: there is a liveliness to it.

**EH**: The metaphor is like the Berlin Wall – where one side of it is completely covered in graffiti, and the other side is immaculate because nobody is allowed to touch it. The building provides a lightning rod and it forces people to show their hand. You're absolutely right that it is a myth that 'community' means that everybody gets on; actually, 'community' means that everyone helps fix the roof, but it doesn't mean that they are pals.

**AF**: It is exactly the same when you look back at the religious community; it was certainly not a 'holier than thou' atmosphere. Some of the young seminarians would put bets on the horses on a Friday afternoon, which would be sneaked off site by the gardener's family.

One of the very odd things about St Peter's is that at some times it was better known on the other side of the world than it was within ten square miles of the building. It almost became invisible, on a local level, apart from to a few people who hadn't been put off by the enclosed nature of the woods, or the reputation of the nefarious activities going on within the seminary in its abandoned form. But it has also existed as a national and international story, where people in the art and architectural community know the narrative of the building very well. It is very interesting to work with and widen the definition of community.

**EH**: It has had a sort of mythical status, hasn't it? By being 'apparently' inaccessible, but then for the local people, who could access it, it was 'not there', it was just a sort of 'hole'.

**AF**: NVA are taking on this complexity, and it represents a very optimistic step. As everyone searches for terms for what they are doing, I keep coming back to this notion of the 'productive', which Alan Pert introduced: productive art and productive landscape, and what that means. It is slightly utopian, because 'production' by its very nature means the act of bringing forth, of producing knowledge, of producing the new form that comes out of the restored building and landscape. In a wider sense it is an attempt to move beyond passive consumerism, and to let the people who come know,

at certain times, that there is the opportunity to do more, and that that is inherently a good thing.

**EH**: People go to arts centres for a day out when it is raining, and to get a nice cappuccino ... that is effectively like going and walking around Ikea and looking at the kitchens, because it doesn't produce anything, or it relies on production by a very tight body of professionals. That is so different from asking people to do something, which we are not used to. With work you are given your money and you give over your time, and there is a sort of exchange. But beyond that, people doing things, it is not easy to get people to do that, because you're asking overlapping communities, very different communities. And visitors who might come for a day, or who might be coming for six months. But in a sense that's what monasteries and friaries used to do, to some extent: there was always the old lady who came to do the flowers, and there were always monks who painted the ritual habit again and again ...

**AF**: I'd say people could overlap in an unselfconscious way, and that is a tricky state to maintain, but that is a particular holy grail. It's also important that we don't see what we offer as the most important thing, and for everyone to be precious around what is being delivered. Sometimes it might be about the opposite – taking the skills out of the site to assist with particular local problems. In Cardross, for example, they are fighting to keep the library alive. One of the most powerful things that has arisen from local dialogues, is that a number of interest groups are beginning to emerge. We would facilitate rather than lead those groups to, for example, collect mementoes from the history of Kilmahew / St Peter's that might be found in personal collections, gathering dust in people's attics, on the other side of the world. We've been sent a reference to a curling ball that was inscribed and slid across the ice in 1901 for the opening of the curling pond in Kilmahew Woods. Mementoes like this can be brought in, and then the local library can become a focus and a resource to document them, and become a new hub of evidence, an archive, as it builds up.

EH: The temptation would be to suggest 'you can put your library in our hands, and we will sort it out for you', but actually that's not the point.

AF: The other aspect of the education programme, which I suppose drives it for me, is that over the last ten years, I've been pulled into lots of seminars, workshops, conferences and symposia in various academic institutions that sometimes generate really good new thinking, but often present it in an over-concentrated form. I think too much is attempted in too short a period of time. Books or papers are produced, which are disseminated within academic networks, but that information doesn't necessarily go out into the wider world. The arts and humanities have been particularly weak in that sense. Although we are on one level hoping to make another small, isolated set up, the aim within it would be to bring some of that great and groundbreaking thinking out and make it available for people in surroundings that are themselves inherently inspirational. The work and the setting will theoretically generate a strong way of gaining new insight.

EH: Once upon a time as an academic you'd write four papers in as many years, and as long as they had an ISB number attached to them it was marvellous. Now they want you to show that someone has read it and acted upon it, gone and done something, so it's changed their world. How have you influenced someone's behaviour? Everyone is running around to try to prove this!

AF: So the importance here is the external partnerships. St Peter's can position itself effectively as a conduit for people who might be interested in a whole range of specialised subjects, which you bring back into the landscape and root by using physical evidence related to theory or findings.

EH: There is nothing like a place to do that, because places make you think. It was great that we discussed this in Venice; that is the sort of place that forces you to think about what cities are and what buildings are, because it is so weird. That is what

St Peter's can do: work as a site that forces you to think about the relationship of buildings to nature, the relationship of various visions of landscape to buildings and time, programme and structure. As you say, those things become teaching devices.

AF: The thinking is that you would have a lead academic discipline each year, so each season of research is led by a particular line of inquiry within an invited network of participating institutions. Then, come the summer, the outcomes of this research are disseminated with a force of imagination through [artists'] commissions, but all driven from the core perspective of that discipline. The interpretation would change the next year, so you are not creating a point of stasis. As fresh channels of thinking arise and as knowledge accrues and changes, the invited feedback from the public within those programmes will keep revealing new perspectives on the site and our place within it.

EH: This steers away from the whole tradition of gardens being didactic, where for instance the temple in the landscape means something specific and you walk around it and it tells you what to think. There's also a tradition of gardens as sites of temporary events, like Versailles, which emerged out of a sequence of parties, each of which lasted over three days every May for twenty years [that's how the gardens built up: as relics of these parties, through amazing installation events]. What you then do is layer that landscape, because the interpretation of it varies each year. The landscape itself will be changing, and the state of the building will be changing. It will be fascinating. Because it is an extruded section, the temptation of the seminary building is that you just fill in the next arch, or the next archive; that would be like honeybees filling it up!

AF: Yes, it is a wonderful battle between idealism and practicality.

EH: So, when the building control officer actually comes round and says, 'Is it finished yet?', you can say, 'Yes, in about 40 years and I don't know what it's going to look like'.

There have been many architectural utopian models in the past based on the infinitely extendable building; the British Library in London, for example, has this idea to extend indefinitely along railway tracks. But what is so hard is the building industry, planning industry and funders all asking what the result will be, while really you are trying not to get painted into a corner.

AF: One of the challenges is to avoid that sense you get with quite a lot of historic landscapes where it is like coming back to an old friend. It gives the false comfort that you think you understand the perspective that built it, because it all becomes too readable.

EH: At the end of the Futurist Manifesto they state that the oldest of them is thirty years old, so they have ten years in which to finish their work, before the young come and take them away! It is a difficult model to build on, but in a sense one can be assured that the future will be unpredictable, and that is a great thing.

In 1992 I visited a beautiful garden in Sri Lanka built by architect Geoffrey Bawa in the 1950s. It looked like he had worked on it for 200 years. He'd built all the walls and foundations so that they burst open with all the roots coming out, and he'd never cut the grass, so it felt like a lawn that had grown over, and every building was like a ruined pavilion, a raw wilderness with buildings that had been demolished.

AF: Was it seen as a radical exercise, or a romantic exercise?

EH: For him it was a romantic exercise, because he wanted it to maintain itself in that state all the time. But that seemingly unloved state in a process of decay actually had to be incredibly carefully maintained, so it was a manicured artform.

AF: Given the monumentality of the forms at St Peter's, there's an assumption that there is a rawness and a vitality in that brutal, exposed concrete form that will gravitate away from a more direct romantic reading. Or maybe it's just a nuanced romanticism?

EH: A lot of the mythologising of St Peter's over time is actually deeply romantic. I think we are allowed to be romantic about modernism, because its tale is so tragic.

This conversation took place mid-June 2011.

# Postscripts

These comments were written upon return from and after further reflection on the debate.

Anyone needing convincing of the possibilities [of Kilmahew / St Peter's] should be directed to Murray Grigor's rapturous, elegaic film *Space and Light Revisited*. Revisiting the ruin that was once a utopian space, the filmmaker shows how it is possible to explore sensitively the complex dynamics of architectural intention, spiritual purpose and cultural legacy. Grigor offers his viewers no settled view, no consolation. That is how it should be. St Peter's is a troublesome, troubling place, but it is also one of the nation's most compelling and charismatic places. As such, it demands our continuing care, interpretation and experimentation.

*Hayden Lorimer*

The commission plan completed last year [by NVA] sets out a variety of options for the transformation of the buildings and 140 acres of semi-ancient woodlands. This was the first time anyone had drawn serious attention to the significance of the landscape. For the first time the opportunities for the seminary building and the site shifted away from a developer-led set of principles to an approach which focuses on the landscape's character. Ecology, heritage, conservation, preservation, restoration are all explored and understood as part of a plan to creatively transform the site and the building. The archaeology of ideas, which have developed over the last two years through investigation, consultation, discussion and imaginative thinking, sets out a vision for a distinctive creative process and offers great potential for the site within a local and national context.

*Alan Pert*

NVA's ideas for St Peter's are very much rooted in their interdisciplinary practice, the interface between architecture, visual art and community development. St Peter's is an international asset, of interest to the world - not just our wee patch of it - and the potential for using it to showcase world best practice in public art and conservation is huge.

*Hayden Lorimer*

Venice reminds us powerfully of the beauty but also the frailty of heritage. Venice is heritage par excellence. As conservationists in the 1980s, we debated and dissected the Venice Charter, whose exponents demanded adherence without compromise. The debate has moved on to a less passionate, more technical level, but it was good to talk about the future of conservation in such a place, where it remains a vitally important issue.

We saw that OMA and others had chosen the Biennale to examine preservation, particularly of post-war architecture, which is so full of philosophical difficulties. They also ask an interesting question about whether 'forwardness' and development should pay for 'backwardness' and preservation in a kind of cultural set-aside arrangement.

Watching the films *Space and Light* and *Space and Light Revisited* side by side, and hearing the comments from an international audience, I think we all realised that conserving a twentieth-century architectural masterpiece in a beautiful designed landscape is not a uniquely Scottish issue, but a universal one.

*Ranald MacInnes*

Kilmahew suggests a condensed history: all components now ruined but still emblematic, romantic and heroic in their original ambitions to create better ways to live. The ruins – including St Peter's – should be left or stabilised as visitor attractions: for contemplation, inspiration and historical reference. Within this extraordinary and slightly post-apocalyptic vision of lost worlds, a new vision should be developed for a better way to live and work; new buildings, new gardens, new social systems, drawn from the multiple communities and cultures of the area, led by creative and visionary people – an experimental, educational and utopian grand folly.

*Adam Sutherland*

# To Have and To Hold
## Ian Gilzean

Responding directly to curator Kazuyo Sejima's theme for the 12th Venice Architecture Biennale, the relationship between people and architecture – and in particular architectural heritage – was at the heart of Scotland's contribution to the Biennale.

To Have and To Hold, curated by NVA and supported by the Scottish Government, Creative Scotland and the British Council, debated the proposed creative re-use of Gillespie, Kidd & Coia's now derelict modern masterpiece, the St Peter's Seminary at Cardross. The exploration of a new set of possibilities for the Kilmahew site was very much in tune with wider themes of heritage and preservation filtering through many pavilions at the Biennale, including a major installation on this topic by Rem Koolhaas and OMA in the Italian Pavilion. A key element of the Scottish programme was the screening of Murray Grigor's film Space and Light Revisited in the Santa Maria Ausiliatrice. This neighbourhood church was ideally located on the route between the main Biennale sites at the Arsenale and the Giardini, and provided an intimate yet accessible setting for the film. Space and Light Revisited provided a dramatic and moving backdrop for a wide-ranging debate about the future of the

seminary building within the context of the wider landscape setting of the Kilmahew site. Through the commissioning plan funded by Creative Scotland, NVA's approach is to consider the landscape setting and the seminary building as a whole, in order to find a way forward based on a deep understanding of the history as well as the social and cultural context of the site. During the discussions in Venice, there was general agreement that a new approach was needed, given that previous attempts to return the seminary building to something of its former glory had come to nothing. NVA's strategy recognises the inherent power not only in the human history of the site, its surroundings and the physical form of the building itself, but also in the processes that have brought them to their present condition.

I feel that we are now moving from a position of knowing that something must be done (but not really knowing what that might be) to a new position that accepts the present condition of the building and recasts our relationship with it. It is now vitally important to invest time in research and careful consideration of the appropriate kind and level of intervention. For many years, the

building deteriorated through passive neglect, but we are now moving, at last, to a position of active engagement. This engagement may be modest at first, and it may be incremental, but what is important is that, following the Venice debate and the transfer of the missives from the Archdiocese of Glasgow to NVA, a new journey has begun.

Another more practical advantage of this incremental approach is that it enables the gradual stabilisation and restoration of the remaining seminary structure to take place while safe access is opened up and routes through and into the landscape are generated. Moreover, by creatively re-imagining Kilmahew as a public landscape and developing a programme of public art, teaching and research to take place within the site, there is the possibility of creating a positive dialogue around the challenges of restoration, which will have an international resonance.

What repeatedly captivated both the eye and the mind in Murray Grigor's film was the dramatic relationship between the site, the surrounding landscape and the building itself. The challenge now for NVA is to deliver a project which exploits

this dramatic potential while involving the local community and the people of Scotland more widely. If this can be done successfully – and, at the same time, attract international interest – then I believe a radical new form of public art will be created which can be of great cultural value.

To have taken the debate to Venice has been valuable in a number of ways. It has revealed the wider relevance and pertinence of the issues with which we are concerned. More than this, the consensus of views expressed in an international forum helped to test and validate the path that NVA has chosen, helping to clearly frame challenges in the context of further debate here in Scotland.

Following the Biennale event and the transfer of the missives from the Archdiocese, Creative Scotland has provided further funding to enable NVA and its team to fully engage in the process of developing the masterplan and artistic programme and, importantly, begin a major fundraising campaign. It is clear that the talks in Venice did a great deal to reinforce belief in this new approach, which after years of neglect, may enable real and positive change to take place on the ground at Cardross.

# Contributors and Debate Participants

**John Allan** - London, UK
www.avantiarchitects.co.uk
John Allan is Director of Avanti Architects and was first Chairman of DoCoMoMo-UK. He has undertaken restoration projects on a wide range of buildings including those by Lubetkin, Goldfinger, Wells Coates, Connell Ward & Lucas, Maxwell Fry and Patrick Gwynne. His publications include *Berthold Lubetkin – Architecture and the Tradition of Progress* (1992), 'The Conservation of Modern Buildings' in *Building Maintenance and Preservation* (1994) and 'Points of Balance – Patterns of Practice in the Conservation of Modern Architecture' in *Conservation of Modern Architecture* (2007). He serves on the London Advisory Committee of English Heritage and is Visiting Professor in Conservation at the University of Sheffield.

**Morag Bain** - Glasgow, UK
Morag Bain works within Architecture and Design Scotland's ACCESS to Architecture Programme, managing a programme of exhibitions, education, events, as well as the website. Coming from a multi-disciplinary background she has practised in art and worked in theatre, architecture and teaching.

**Leonardo Ciacci** – Venice, Italy
Leonardo Ciacci is Associate Professor in Urbanism at the Faculty of Architecture at the IUAV University in Venice, where he teaches on Urbanism and Urban Theory. He is particularly interested in the representation of architecture and the urban realm and its communication through film. He has written numerous publications on architecture and produced a range of film and video projects on the subject.

**Emma Cocker** – Nottingham, UK
not-yet-there.blogspot.com
Emma Cocker is a writer, artist and Senior Lecturer in Fine Art at Nottingham Trent University. Her practice is characterised by a state of restlessness or wandering that serves as both subject and motivation. She is increasingly interested in performative, invitational, propositional and even cartographic models for the production of texts. Processes of extraction, fragmentation, listing, footnoting and cross-referencing have become critical methods for attempting to produce 'openings' rather than drawing conclusions, or for appearing purposeful while remaining without clear or discernible intent. Emma is co-editor of *Transmission: Speaking and Listening*, a collaborative project between Site Gallery and Sheffield Hallam University.

**David Cook** – Glasgow, UK
www.waspsstudios.org.uk
David Cook is Chief Executive of Wasps Artists' Studios, an arts social enterprise that specialises in creating and managing affordable workspace for the cultural and creative industries across Scotland. Wasps is one of the largest organisations of its kind in Europe, supporting 750 artists each year at nineteen urban, rural and island locations, with a £1.5m annual turnover and £5m in assets. David is currently board member for the Cultural Enterprise Office and CESEL Services Ltd (a community social enterprise in Kelso), and Chair of NVA.

**Angus Farquhar** - Glasgow, UK
www.nva.org.uk
Angus Farquhar gained a degree in English and Drama
at Goldsmiths College, University of London, before
going on to perform for ten years as a core member
of Test Dept, a radical music collective based in South
London. Returning to Scotland in 1989, he re-initiated
the Beltane Fire Festival in Edinburgh, Europe's largest fire
festival. Angus is Creative Director of NVA, a public arts
charity based in Glasgow. Since NVA's inception in 1992,
Angus has produced and directed NVA's temporary and
permanent public artworks and events. NVA's vision is to
make powerful public art, which articulates the complex
qualities of a location through collective action. The work
is ambitious, inspirational and internationalist, seeing each
audience member as an individual who, through direct
experience, is enriched and inspired in their own beliefs
and values.

**Ian Gilzean** - Edinburgh, UK
www.scotland.gov.uk/Topics/Built-Environment/AandP
Ian Gilzean graduated from Edinburgh University School of
Architecture in 1982, and worked in architectural practice
for a number of public sector organisations, in private
practice and in community design units in Wester Hailes,
Edinburgh and Drumchapel, Glasgow. Between 1994 and
1999, he worked for the Scottish Arts Council on its Capital
Arts Programme, funded by the National Lottery. He joined
the then Scottish Executive in 1999 as a Senior Architect
in the Chief Architect's Office and in 2006 assumed his
current post of Chief Architect for the Directorate for the
Built Environment. Ian is responsible for the development
and implementation of the Scottish Government's policy
on architecture. He is an External Examiner for Canterbury
School of Architecture and the Architects Registration
Board (ARB). Ian is visiting Professor at the University of
Strathclyde's Department of Architecture.

**Murray Grigor** - Edinburgh, UK
en.wikipedia.org/wiki/Murray_Grigor
Murray Grigor is internationally renowned for his films on
architecture, which include award-winning works on Frank
Lloyd Wright, John Lautner, Charles Rennie Mackintosh,
Alexander 'Greek' Thomson, and the landmark series
*Pride of Place* – an eight-part PBS series on American
architecture with Robert A. M. Stern. Murray's films on
St Peter's Seminary, *Space and Light* (1972), and *Space
and Light Revisited* (2009) were shown as part of NVA's
presentation at the Venice Biennale 2010.

**Edward Hollis** - Edinburgh, UK
www.edwardhollis.com
Edward Hollis studied architecture at Cambridge and
Edinburgh Universities before working for Richard Murphy
Architects on a series of projects, varying from house
extensions to the transformation of a medieval tollbooth
into a modern music centre. Ed currently runs the Interior
Design department at Edinburgh College of Art. His first
book, *The Secret Lives of Buildings*, was published in 2009.

**Moira Jeffrey** - Glasgow, UK
http://scotlandonsunday.scotsman.com
Moira Jeffrey is a journalist, researcher and visual arts
consultant based in Glasgow. She is currently art critic for
*Scotland on Sunday* and is a prominent features journalist
and reviewer in both print and broadcast media. She
presented the BBC documentary *Hanging in Parliament* on
the controversial art programme conceived for the Scottish
Parliament building. Recent print catalogues include
extended interviews with the Paris-based artist Esther
Shalev-Gerz and the Polish sculptor Monika Sosnowska.
Moira is a former solicitor with degrees in Art History and
Politics, and Scots Law.

**Tilman Latz** – Kranzberg, Germany
www.latzundpartner.de
Tilman Latz has been a partner with Latz + Partner Landscape Architects' practice since 2001, having gained a degree in landscape architecture at the University of Kassel, with an intermediate year at the Architectural Association in London in 1995–6. Between 1997 and 2001 he worked with Jourda Architectes, Paris.
Latz + Partner are the designers of the Duisburg-Nord Landscape Park. This former industrial wasteland, measuring 200 hectares, has been transformed over a period of more than ten years into a new multifunctional landscape park at the centre of which sits a decommissioned metal works. Spontaneously grown vegetation sits alongside deliberately designed green spaces and garden areas, combining industrial history, nature, recreation, leisure and culture.

**Hayden Lorimer** – Glasgow, UK
www.ges.gla.ac.uk:443/staff/hlorimer
Hayden Lorimer is a cultural geographer and writer, and is currently a Senior Lecturer in the Department of Geographical and Earth Sciences at Glasgow University. The stories he digs up take their forms from landscape, nature, movement, memory and past lives. He has been published widely, across disciplinary fields, and has collaborated with artists, anthropologists and scientists. His essays have been broadcast on BBC radio, most recently the series *Running the World*.

**Ranald MacInnes** – Edinburgh, UK
www.historic-scotland.gov.uk
Ranald is Principal Inspector, South West Team with the Scottish Government's heritage agency, Historic Scotland. He is an honorary Senior Research Fellow of Glasgow University's Institute for Art History and has written several books and articles on Scottish architectural history.

**Henry McKeown** – Glasgow, UK
www.jmarchitects.net
Henry McKeown graduated in 1986 from the Mackintosh School of Architecture, and has practised architecture in Scotland since working first with Nicholas Groves-Raines, then with Elder & Cannon Architects. In 1996 Henry formed a partnership with Ian Alexander (McKeown Alexander Architects) and in 2004 the practice merged with jmarchitects. Since 1998 Henry has been a studio tutor at the Mackintosh School of Architecture and he has lectured widely in Scotland and overseas. In 2009 jmarchitects, in collaboration with Steven Holl Architects (New York), won the commission to design a new building for the Glasgow School of Art opposite the existing Mackintosh building.

**Professor Gordon Murray** – Glasgow, UK
www.gordonmurrayarchitects.com
Gordon Murray is principal of Gordon Murray Architects. Gordon's work has been exhibited at the Royal Institute of British Architects in London, at the Royal Scottish Academy and RIAS in Edinburgh, at the Lighthouse in Glasgow and in the 2004 Venice Biennale. As a commentator on architecture in Scotland he has written for *The Herald*, *The Scotsman* and several architectural publications, as well as broadcasting on radio and television. Gordon was appointed both Professor of Architecture and Urban Design and Head of School at the University of Strathclyde in 2007.

**Professor Alan Pert** – Glasgow, UK
www.nordarchitecture.com
A principal of the Northern Office for Research and Design (NORD), Alan Pert is an architect, educator and researcher. Alan established NORD in June 2002 with fellow director Robin Lee. Prior to NORD, Alan was joint founder of Zoo Architects and a key member of the team working on the Tramway redevelopment project, which won the RIAS Architecture Grand Prix and the RIAS Award for Best Public Building in 2001. Alan is course director at the University of Strathclyde and an Honorary Lecturer at Dundee School of Art. NORD's work has been recognised throughout Europe with projects widely published in international periodicals and newspapers.

**Professor Jane Rendell** – London, UK
www.janerendell.co.uk
Professor Jane Rendell is Director of Architectural Research at the Bartlett, UCL, an architectural designer and historian, art critic and writer. Her work over the past ten years has explored various interdisciplinary intersections: feminist theory and architectural history, fine art and architectural design, autobiographical writing and criticism. She regularly gives talks at galleries such as the Barbican and the Whitechapel, and has recently written essays for artists and architects (including Daniel Arsham, Nathan Coley and Janet Hodgson), galleries (such as the Hayward, the Serpentine and the BALTIC) and projects (such as the Estonian Pavilion and the Venice Architecture Biennale, 2008).

**Rolf Roscher** – Glasgow, UK
www.erzstudio.co.uk
Rolf Roscher is a director of ERZ limited, a dynamic design practice based in Glasgow that specialises in landscape design, urbanism, masterplanning and strategy. ERZ has a strongly collaborative and multidisciplinary approach to landscape design. Rolf has been based in Glasgow since 1993, after having previously worked and taught in Oregon and Australia. Rolf's built projects, including Glasgow's Hidden Gardens and the Matrix and Chroma housing schemes, have won numerous design awards including Civic Trust Awards, Dynamic Places Awards and Scottish Design Awards. Rolf is Chairman of the Hidden Gardens Trust and an Enabler for Architecture and Design Scotland.

**Adam Sutherland** – Cumbria, UK
www.grizedale.org
Adam Sutherland is a director of Grizedale Arts, a rural arts organisation based on a working farm in the Lake District. Under Adam's directorship the organisation has moved from a traditional sculpture park towards a socially focused programme supporting artists in working with the local community, as well as on international projects that are reflective of the local conditions. Recent projects include an enhanced Harvest Festival with the local church, and a representation of the local village hall for the São Paolo Biennale.

**Gerrie van Noord** – London, UK
Gerrie van Noord is a visual arts consultant / curator and has worked on a diversity of projects, ranging from Scotland's first independent presentation at the Venice Biennale for Visual Art in 2003, to Glasgow's first lighting festival *Radiance* in 2005. Gerrie also works as a free-lance editor and publisher. She has been a Visiting Lecturer on the MFA programme at the Glasgow School of Art since 2003, and she is Academic Advisor and Lecturer at the MA Arts Policy and Management at Birkbeck, University of London.

# Image Captions and Credits

P. 7 – Kilmahew Burn. Photo: Gerrie van Noord.

PP. 8 and 9 – Stills from Murray Grigor's films *Space and Light* (1972, left) and *Space and Light Revisited* (2009, right). The images show a view into the (former) refectory.

P. 10 – View towards a bridge over one of the burns with overgrown embankments. Photo: NVA.

P. 11 – The first-floor level of the teaching block, in September 2009. Photo: Gerrie van Noord.

P. 13 – Top: General Roy's map showing 'indication of emparked' landscape circa 1750s – sourced from National Library of Scotland Maps; William Roy Military Survey of Scotland, 1747–55 © The British Library. Licensor www.scran.ac.uk.

Bottom: Kilmahew House in the early 1900s. Photo: Sheena Allan, courtesy Michael Wilson.

P. 14 – View from the drawing room of Kilmahew House into the garden in the early 1900s. Photo: Sheena Allan, courtesy Michael Wilson.

P. 15 – The Swan Pond in its early days. Photo: Sheena Allan, courtesy Michael Wilson.

P. 16 – Kilmahew House and the newly built St Peter's Seminary, in 1968. Photo: Glasgow School of Art Archives and Collections; Gillespie, Kidd & Coia archives.

P. 18 – Tree canopy in Kilmahew Woods. Photo: Neil Davidson.

P. 19 – Map devised for the Exploring Kilmahew walk, October 2010, with temporary signage and bridge. Courtesy NVA.

P. 23 – Walkers discussing the old Kilmahew Castle or Keep during the Exploring Kilmahew walk, in October 2010. Photo: Neil Davidson.

P. 24 – Walkers discovering the terrain during the Exploring Kilmahew walk, in October 2010. Photo: Neil Davidson.

P. 25 – The external concrete staircase, next to the main seminary building. Photo: Angus Farquhar.

P. 26 – The overhang of the teaching block above the gorge, towering over the trees below. Photo: Gerrie van Noord.

P. 27 – The dilapidated glasshouse in the former walled garden. Photo: NVA.

P. 29 – View towards the main seminary building, with the ziggurat roof over the chapel, and the teaching block on the right. Photo: Glasgow School of Art Archives and Collections; Gillespie, Kidd & Coia archives.

P. 31 – Axonometric drawing of the original elements of the seminary. Image courtesy Avanti Architects.

P. 32 – Left: most of the roof beams have disappeared from the chapel since this image was taken, in September 2009. Photo: Gerrie van Noord.

Right: cladding and other material have fallen from the original structure of the teaching block and are clearly visible underneath it, December 2008. Photo: NVA.

P. 33 – Left: view from the edge of the chapel into the former refectory. Photo: Gerrie van Noord.

Right: the top of the light silos along the edge of the main block. Photo: Johnny Bute.

P. 35 – View onto the Grand Canal in Venice from the Accademia Bridge. Photo: Gerrie van Noord.

P. 36 – The seminary building with the light silos, September 2009. Photo: Gerrie van Noord.

P. 37 – The cantilever of the teaching block in the 1960s. The surrounding trees clearly hadn't encroached as extensively as they have now. Photo: Glasgow School of Art Archives and Collections; Gillespie, Kidd & Coia archives.

PP. 38–48 – All colour images of the May Morn house on the right-hand pages by Jane Rendell. All scans of black and white images on the left-hand pages of found magazines in the ruins of May Morn courtesy Jane Rendell.

P. 50 – View from the end of main block towards the chapel. Photo: Glasgow School of Art Archives and Collections; Gillespie, Kidd & Coia archives.

P. 51 – The convent block, in December 2008. Photo: NVA.

P. 52 – The top of the light silos on the side of the main building: Photo: NVA.

P. 53 – View towards the back wall of the chapel, with the rounded ceilings of the side chapels in the foreground. Photo: Angus Farquhar.

P. 55 – 'Unsightly aids' supporting a wall along Sestiere Dorsoduro in Venice, July 2011. Photo: Gerrie van Noord.

P. 56 – Layers of cladding hanging from the teaching block ceiling, February 2008. Photo: NVA.

P. 57 – The staircase in the main building block, in September 2009. Photo: Gerrie van Noord.

P. 58 – View towards farmland from Kilmahew Wood. Photo: Gerrie van Noord.

P. 59 – View of one of the burns cutting through the wider estate. Photo: Neil Davidson.

P. 60 – The temporary bridge installed for the Exploring Kilmahew walk, in October 2010. Photo: Neil Davidson.

P. 61 – View towards the rhododendrons on the island in the Swan Pond. Photo: NVA.

P. 63 – One of the structures in the Bosco dei Mostri in Bomarzo in Italy. Photo: Latz + Partner.

P. 64 – View over various planted areas in Duisburg-Nord. Photo: Rolf Roscher.

P. 65 – The former blast furnaces in Duisburg-Nord. Photo: Latz + Partner.

P. 66 – Overgrown former industrial structures in Duisburg-Nord. Photo: Latz + Partner.

P. 67 – A view across the former Kilmahew estate, with the seminary building wrapped around Kilmahew House. Photo taken before Kilmahew House was demolished in 1995. Photo: Guthrie Aerial Photography.

P. 68 – The former walled garden, in September 2009. Photo: Gerrie van Noord.

P. 72 – The writing's on the wall: a sprayed statement on a bridge banister pillar. Photo: Johnny Bute.

P. 73 – View through Kilmahew Wood. Photo: Neil Davidson.

P. 75 – Top: a volunteer helps clear an overgrown path. Photo: NVA.

Bottom, left: a family resting under a tree during the Exploring Kilmahew walk in October 2010. Photo: Neil Davidson.

Bottom, right: whin dyke, September 2009. Photo: Gerrie van Noord.

P. 77 – South-East entrance gate to the former walled garden. Photo: Neil Davidson.

PP. 78–9 – The rhododendron tunnel on the western edge of the woods. Photo: Neil Davidson.

P. 80 – A walker exploring the site during the Exploring Kilmahew walk, in October 2010. Photo: Neil Davidson.

P. 81 – A line of trees showing off their late autumn splendour, in 2008. Photo: NVA.

P. 82 – The altar in the former chapel of the main building. Photo: James Johnson.

P. 83 – Walkers tracing the paths during the Exploring Kilmahew walk, in October 2010. Photo: Neil Davidson.

P. 84 – Where teaching block and seminary building meet, December 2008. Photo: NVA.

P. 85 – Temporary shelter during the Exploring Kilmahew walk, in October 2010. Photo: Neil Davidson.

P. 86 – View towards the seminary building from the convent block, December 2008. Photo: NVA.

P. 86 – The convent block in December 2008. Photo: NVA.

P. 94 – The big redwood tree. Photo: Neil Davidson

P. 95 – Map courtesy ERZ Ltd.

P. 97 – Food, fun and wayfinding during the Exploring Kilmahew walk, in October 2010.
All photos: Neil Davidson.

P. 99 – Altar underneath beams (which have now all but disappeared) in the former chapel, autumn 2008.
Photo: NVA.

PP. 102–3 – View into the former refectory in the main building, in December 2008. Photo: NVA.

P. 104 – The foundations of the former Kilmahew House (demolished in 1995), in 2008. Photo: NVA.

P. 105 – The remains of the roof of the former teaching block, December 2008. Photo: NVA.

P. 109 – View from the gorge towards the teaching block cantilever, in October 2010. Photo: Neil Davidson.

P. 110 – View towards the teaching block, in December 2008. Photo: Angus Farquhar.

P. 111 – The top of the light silos along the main building, in December 2008. Photo: NVA.

P. 112 – The debate in Venice, November 2010, moderated by Gordon Murray (in centre with black glasses).
Photo: Roman Tcherpak, Venice.

P. 118 – Edward Hollis talking during the debate. Photo: Roman Tcherpak, Venice.

P. 119 – Angus Farquhar (left), Gerrie van Noord (middle) and Adam Sutherland (seen from back).
Photo: Roman Tcherpak, Venice.

P. 120 – David Cook (just visible on left), Rolf Roscher (middle) and Tilman Latz (right).
Photo: Roman Tcherpak, Venice.

P. 121 – Pensive faces during the debate in Venice, with from left to right Henry McKeown, Alan Pert,
Leonardo Ciacci, Moira Jeffrey, Ranald MacInnes (seen from back) and Edward Hollis. Photo: Roman
Tcherpak, Venice.

# With Special Thanks to:

Murray Grigor for making both *Space and Light* (1972) and *Space and Light Revisited* (2009) available for screening on various occasions, including in Venice, in November 2010.

Ian Gilzean, Les Scott and the Scottish Government for their invitation to and support for the NVA presentation at the 12th Architecture Biennale in Venice in 2010.

Amanda Catto and Iain Munro for ongoing support from Creative Scotland.

Vicky Richardson, British Council, London.

All those who participated in and attended the debate in Venice in November 2010, and / or have contributed to this publication, including Morag Bain, Leonardo Ciacci, Emma Cocker, David Cook, Angus Farquhar, Ian Gilzean, Murray Grigor, Edward Hollis, Moira Jeffrey, Iris Latz, Tilman Latz, Hayden Lorimer, Ranald MacInnes, Henry McKeown, Iain Munro, Gordon Murray, Alan Pert, Jane Rendell, Sandy Robinson, Rolf Roscher, Adam Sutherland and Gerrie van Noord.

Angie Bual for practical arrangements, Cara Connolly for her film created from the debate, and M+B Studio srl, Venice, for the arrangements in and around the debate location, the Santa Maria Ausiliatrice.

All residents from Renton and Cardross, for their collaboration, curiosity and feedback during planning days, walks and workshops in the last two years.

Clare Hunter for her consultancy work on Community Development, and Chris Hughes for his role as Community Development Officer 2010, funded by Argyll & Bute Leader Programme.

Avanti Architects for their support in providing drawings and images.

ERZ Ltd for their support and provision of maps and images.

PAR+RS for their report on the Venice debate and their permission to republish Gordon Murray's text.

Michael Wilson for making available Sheena Allan's photographs of Kilmahew House in the early 1900s.

Carol Hogel for her ongoing support to NVA.

# Colophon

*To Have and To Hold*
*Future of a Contested Landscape*

Published by NVA, Glasgow and
Luath Press Ltd, Edinburgh

The text by Gordon Murray was originally published on
the Public Art Scotland (PAR+RS) website at
http://www.publicartscotland.com/reflections/68.

The text by Edward Hollis was previously published in
the brochure produced prior to the debate in Venice in
November 2010. The full brochure can be downloaded
from http://www.nva.org.uk/pdf/VENICE_PROGRAMME_
FINAL_compressed.pdf.

Jane Rendell's and Emma Cocker's texts have been laid out
to their specifications.

ISBN: 978-1-908373-10-6

Editor: Gerrie van Noord
Assistant Editor: Nicola Godsal
Proofer: Tim West
Designer: Susie Simmons
Repro: Dexter Premedia
Printing and binding: Stewarts of Edinburgh

NVA
15 North Claremont Street
Glasgow G3 7NR
Tel: +44 (0)141 332 9911
contact@nva.org.uk
www.nva.org.uk

NVA team: Angus Farquhar, Ellen Potter, Nicola Godsal,
Jon Clarke and Adam Scarborough

Luath Press Ltd
543 / 2 Castlehill
The Royal Mile
Edinburgh EH1 2ND
Tel + 44 (0)131 225 4326
sales@luath.co.uk
www.luath.co.uk

Luath Press Ltd team: Gavin MacDougall, Robin Jones,
Hannah Sim and Christine Wilson

www.nva.org.uk          www.luath.co.uk

NVA is a registered charity (SC02763) and is supported
by Creative Scotland.

This publication is published with support from Creative
Scotland, the British Council and The Scottish Government

www.creativescotland.com          www.scotland.gov.uk

www.britishcouncil.org